COME AWAY MY BELOVED

KING'S FARSPAN, INC.
1473 So. La Luna Avenue
Ojai, California 93023

Books by Frances J. Roberts

Come Away, My Beloved
This book will help you find the quiet place of communion, sense the presence of God and respond to His overtures. A six-part compilation of the six booklets listed below.

Booklets
Lovest Thou Me?　　　*Learn to Reign*
Living Water　　　　*Listen to the Silence*
Launch Out!　　　　*The Sounding of the Trumpet*

Total Love
A companion book to "Come Away, My Beloved." Fresh food for the soul. Encouraging, Holy Spirit-anointed. Pertinent message for today's challenges.

Dialogues with God
Devotional writings. Similar to "Come Away, My Beloved."

Make Haste, My Beloved
A tender but insistent call from the heart of God to the heart of His people. It is a call to purity: a light illuminating our path. A book you will read today and keep forever.

On the Highroad of Surrender
A choice spiritual feast awaits you in this book which plumbs the depths and scales the heights of divine revelation. Inspiring and practical.

Progress of Another Pilgrim
Challenging, inspirational. A thrilling sequel to "Come Away, My Beloved" and "Dialogues with God."

Angel in the Fire
A beautiful book on death, grief and eternal life. Gift quality, with four full page pictorial illustrations.

Christmas Reflections
A compilation of Frances J. Roberts' writings, poems and songs on the Advent theme. Parchment. Illustrated. Gift book.

O Wondrous Love
A long-play stereo record of ten beautiful songs with words and music by Frances J. Roberts.

Published by KING'S FARSPAN, INC.
1473 S. La Luna Ave., Ojai, California 93023

COME AWAY MY BELOVED

Frances J. Roberts

I LOVEST THOU ME? Page 7

II LIVING WATER Page 33

III LAUNCH OUT! Page 65

IV LEARN TO REIGN Page 97

V LISTEN TO THE SILENCE Page 129

VI THE SOUNDING OF THE TRUMPET Page 161

Illustrated by Marjorie Nordwall

34th Printing

836,000 Copies Sold

Deluxe gift edition: ISBN 0-932814-05-0
Hardcover edition: ISBN 0-932814-01-8
Softcover edition: ISBN 0-932814-02-6

Preface

Come Away, My Beloved was forged in the crucible of life. In the midst of each day's joys and trials has come the ministering spirit of the Heavenly Father and the Lord Jesus Christ, bringing words of encouragement, hope, comfort and conviction.

To gain the maximum blessing from this book, read it carefully and prayerfully, a little at a time, searching always for the special treasure of truth for your own need. He who knows you by name and understands your deepest longings will speak to your heart from these pages, shutting out the world about you and bringing you into fellowship with Himself.

Whether you are just beginning your Christian walk or have grown into a fuller stature in Christ, you will be equally challenged and helped. Some books give instruction for Christian living; others inspire to greater devotion. *Come Away, My Beloved* will do both as you open your soul to its living message.

With this book go many prayers that God will enrich every life it touches. Surely we are all bound together in one family in Christ through the bonds of His Holy Spirit.

—FJR

This book is dedicated to the glory of God
and to all who desire a closer walk with Him.

LOVEST THOU ME?

". . . Jesus saith to Simon Peter, Simon, son of Jonas, lovest thou me more than these? He saith unto him, Yea, Lord; thou knowest that I love thee. He saith unto him, Feed my lambs."

John 21:15

Contents

The Call of Love 13
The Need For Greater Faith 13
Resignation 14
Faith And Action 14
Sincerity 15
Guidance 15
On the Waters of Sorrow 16
Set Thy Course By My Promises 16
Dependence On God 17
The Burden Bearer 17
Safety In God's Will 18
Release Thy Grief 18
Ministering Angels 19
Walk On With Me 19
The Vineyard of Prayer 20
A Yielded, Believing Vessel 21
Cherish My Words 22
Comfort In Affliction 22
Return Unto Me 23
One Day At a Time 24
The Blessings of the Pure in Heart 25
The Healing Power of Joy 26
The Divine Commission 28
Sacrifice, My Status Symbol 29
Eternity And Time 31

The Call of Love

O My beloved, abide under the shelter of the lattice — for I have betrothed thee unto Myself, and though ye are sometimes indifferent toward Me, My love for thee is at all times as a flame of fire. My ardor never cools. My longing for thy love and affection is deep and constant.

Tarry not for an opportunity to have more time to be alone with Me. Take it, though ye leave the tasks at hand. Nothing will suffer. Things are of less importance than ye think. Our time together is like a garden full of flowers, whereas the time ye give to things is as a field full of stubble.

I love thee, and if ye can always, as it were, feel My pulse-beat, ye shall know many things the knowledge of which shall give thee sustaining strength. I bare thy sins and I wish to carry thy burdens. Ye may have the gift of a light and merry heart. My love bower is the place where ye shall find it, for My love dispels all fear and is a cure for every ill. Lay thy head upon My breast and lose thyself in Me. Thou shalt experience resurrection life and peace; the joy of the Lord shall become thy strength; and wells of salvation shall be opened within thee.

The Need For Greater Faith

O My child, do not expect the trials to be lighter than in the past. Why should ye think the testings would be less severe? Lo, I prove all things, and there are areas of thy life that I have not touched as yet. Do not look for respite. The days ahead may call for greater endurance and more robust faith than ye have ever needed before. Welcome this, for ye must surely know by this time how precious are the lessons learned through such experiences. If it is not fully possible to anticipate them with joy, it is certainly not difficult to gain an appropriate appreciation of them afterwards, in retrospect.

Apply thine heart to learn wisdom. This goal transcends every other aim, and any other good that comes out of a pressure period is an added blessing in excess.

Seek Me above all else.

Resignation

Incline thine heart unto Me, and let thine ear be attuned to My voice. For lo, I would speak to thee, and I have an urgent message to give thee.

Go not about to establish thine own designs. Lo, I have already set in motion My divine will and purpose and I would not have thee interfere. I am jealous about My children: Lo, they are Mine, saith the Lord; and ye shall not intrude in any way such as would hinder My plans from working out. Yea, ye may do many things, but only that which I direct thee to do can have My blessing upon it.

Resign all into My hands — thy loved ones as well as thine own self. Be obedient to the still small voice. Thine own imaginings may speak more loudly, but wait upon Me always. Ye shall see the wisdom and the glory in this in due time. Fret not about carnal things, but concern thyself first and always about spiritual values. Truly, My promise is still: 'Seek ye FIRST the Kingdom of God, and all the other needful things SHALL BE ADDED unto thee.'

Faith And Action

My promises are of no avail to thee except as ye apply and appropriate them by faith. In thy daily walk, ye shall be victorious only to the degree that ye trust Me. I can help thee only as ye ask. I shall meet you at every point where ye put action alongside thy prayers. Only as ye WALK shall the waters of adversity be parted before thee. Overburdened as the world is with trouble and sickness, I need those who have proved My sufficiency in everyday, personal experience to lead the suffering to the fountains of life. I need those who have found Me as burden-bearer to help bring deliverance to the oppressed.

Never begrudge time given to chronic complainers, but recognize in each encounter the opportunity to speak a word that may lead to their liberation. No case is too hard for Me. Never be taken by surprise when I use you to change a pattern. Do not judge a man by what he appears to be, but see him as what he CAN be if he give himself unreservedly to Me.

Sincerity

Marvel not that I have said that ye must be born anew. Of the flesh, nothing that is spiritual can ever be produced. Spiritual life shall bring forth that which is spiritual; and likewise, carnal flesh shall bring forth only more carnality.

This is why I said I loathed your sacrifices. It was not that I despised the ordinance in itself, but that I perceived that it was a product of the flesh — an expression of self-righteousness and indifference to the claim of God upon thy heart.

My ordinances are good and holy, but they are to be entered into with deep sincerity and with awareness of their true significance. To sacrifice in carelessness and ignorance is to damage thine own soul. Let thy spirit never become callous.

Without holiness, no man shall see God. This could be as truly stated, 'Without a tender heart and sensitive, attentive spirit, none shall see God', for without these, no true holiness will ever be attained.

The fool shall not discern the value, and shall cast aside great treasure. The practiced eye knoweth the true worth of a gem and shall not let it escape him. Thus shall ye be in spiritual matters.

Train thine eye to discern that which is of true worth, and let it not escape thee.

Guidance

My child, hear My voice, and give no heed to the voice of the stranger. My paths are straight, and they are narrow, but ye shall have no difficulty in finding them if ye watch Me. I am guiding thee. Ye need not look to man for direction. Ye may learn much by fellowship with the saints, but never allow any to take the part that is rightfully Mine — to direct thy steps. As it is written, 'The steps of a good man are ORDERED BY THE LORD' — not by the preacher, not by some Christian worker, but by the Lord.

Trust Me to do it, and give Me the time and the opportunity to do it. Be not hasty, and lean not upon thine own intelligence.

Rest in Me. I shall bring to pass My perfect will in thy life as ye believe and live in faith.

On the Waters of Sorrow

O My child, I am coming to thee walking upon the waters of the sorrows of thy life; yea, above the sounds of the storm ye shall hear My voice calling thy name.

Ye are never alone, for I am at thy right hand. Never despair, for I am watching over and caring for thee. Be NOT anxious. What seemeth to thee to be at present a difficult situation is all part of My planning, and I am working out the details of circumstances to the end that I may bless thee and reveal Myself to thee in a new way.

As I have opened thine eyes to see, so shall I open thine ears to hear, and ye shall come to know Me even as did Moses, yea, in a face-to-face relationship.

For I shall remove the veil that separates Me from thee and ye shall know Me as thy dearest Friend and as thy truest Comforter.

No darkness shall hide the shining of My face, for I shall be to thee as a bright star in the night sky. Never let thy faith waver. Reach out thy hand, and thou shalt touch the hem of My garment.

Set Thy Course By My Promises

Be not afraid. I will not allow thine adversaries to swallow thee up. Thou art My child, I shall deliver thee and honor thee and I shall be glorified through thee. Because of My faithfulness unto thee, even thine enemies shall recognize My power. I shall keep thee in sickness, and in death I shall be thy sure comfort. I shall walk with thee through the valley, and thou shalt fear no shadow. Hold to My promises. They are given to thee as a chart is given to a ship, and a compass to the hunter. Ye may set thy course or find thy way by My promises. They will lead thee and guide thee in places where there is no trodden path. They will give thee direction and wisdom and will open up thine own understanding.

Study My Word, the Bible. Lo, it aboundeth with nuggets of courage. They will strengthen thee and help thee, and even in eternity ye shall partake of their far-reaching effects.

Dependence On God

My people, heed My words; yea, walk not carelessly; neither lay out thine own paths on which to travel. Ye cannot know what lieth in the distance, nor what adversity ye may encounter tomorrow. So walk closely with Me, that ye may be able to draw quickly upon My aid. Ye need Me; and no matter how well-developed is thy faith nor how mature is thy growth in grace, never think for a moment that ye need My support any less. Nay, but the truth is that ye need it even more. For I shelter the new-born from many a trial and testing such as I permit to confront those who are growing up in spiritual stature. Yea, verily, ye cannot grow unless I do bring into your lives these proving and testing experiences.

So hold thee more firmly to My hand as ye journey on in thy Christian walk. Trust not in thine own increasing strength; for verily, it is not thy strength but rather My strength within thee that ye feel. Ye are as vulnerable to the treachery of the enemy and as frail as ever; but thy knowledge of Me has deepened, and because of this thy trust in Me should come easier.

Move forward with courage and confidence; but always allow Me to walk ahead, and choose the right path for thee.

The Burden Bearer

My child, do not share thy burdens with all who come unto thee professing concern. Lo, I, Myself, am the great burden-bearer. Ye need not look to another. I will lead thee and guide thee in wisdom from above. All things shall be as I plan them, if ye allow Me the freedom to shape circumstances and lead thee to the right decisions.

I am merciful and kind. I love thee beyond measure. I purpose to do thee good; and lo, I will bring unto thee those who can TRULY help, if ye leave all in My hands.

I want thee to prosper and be in health. I want thee to know Me more intimately. If difficulties come, it is by My order and for thy benefit. Man would say ye have trouble: I would say ye have a test.

Safety In God's Will

My will is not a place, but a condition. Do not ask Me WHERE and WHEN, but ask Me HOW? You will discover blessing in every place, and any place, if thy spirit is in tune with Me. No place nor time is more hallowed than another when ye are truly in love with Me.

I direct every motion of thy life, as the ocean bears a ship. Your will and intelligence may be at the helm, but divine providence and sovereignty are stronger forces. Ye can trust Me, knowing that any pressure I bring to bear upon thy life is initiated by My love, and I will not do even this except as ye are willing and desire.

Many a ship has sailed from port to port with no interference by Me, because Strong Will has been at the wheel. Multitudes of pleasure cruises go merrily in their ways, untouched by the power of My hand.

But ye have put thy life into My keeping, and because ye are depending on Me for guidance and direction, I shall give it.

Move on steadily, and know that the waters that carry thee are the waters of My love and My kindness, and I will keep thee on the right course.

Release Thy Grief

My child, lean thy head upon My bosom. Well I know thy weariness, and every burden I would lift. Never bury thy griefs; but offer them up to Me. Thou wilt relieve thy soul of much strain if ye can lay every care in My hand. Never cling to any trouble, hoping to resolve it thyself, but turn it over to Me; and in doing so, ye shall free Me to work it out.

Ministering Angels

O My soul, be anxious for nothing. It is enough that thy Father loveth thee. Loving thee, He taketh thought of thy smallest need. Surely He will not allow thee to be put to shame, and He will not be unconcerned when ye are in any kind of need.

Turn to Him always, before ye look to any other source of assistance. It is His love that shall light thy path, so that ye may thus be guided in finding other help. Surely He hath given thee ministering angels, and these may sometimes be in the form of thy friends. Accept their ministry as from God, and it shall be doubled in blessing. Ye may also, in turn, be used in similar manner to bless others.

Look not to the physical, alone, for the transmission of spiritual energy. Divine life can flow out to others through thy thoughts, the same as through thy hands. Use My power, and let it flow forth in any form I choose, as I direct and guide you. Ye may multiply thy ministry an hundredfold in this way. Be not restricted by thy present knowledge, but move in and learn more from Me.

Walk On With Me

My child, the path of duty is before thee. It may look rugged, but it is the only way of divine blessing. Choose out some other way, and ye shall find only disappointment and frustration of soul. Weariness shall overtake thee on the smoothest road, if it be not the pathway of my ordained will. Be not deceived by doubts, and be not detained by fears. Move into the center of My purposes for you: ye shall find there are glorious victories waiting for thee, and recompenses far exceeding every sacrifice.

Be obedient: ye shall bring joy to My heart. Neither the applause nor the scorn of men should be of any consequence to thee. My approval is reward enough, and without this, any other satisfaction is not worthy of thy pursuit.

Walk on with Me. I shall be very near to give thee support and encouragement, so ye have nothing to warrant thy fears. They shall vanish as ye obey.

The Vineyard of Prayer

O My child, the days are fraught with burdens that need to be borne upon the shoulders of faithful prayer warriors. Where are the ones who are willing to make themselves available to the Spirit for this ministry? Lo, I say, the Word sown shall dry up like carelessly strewn seed if it be not watered with tears of intercession. Ye cannot in yourself lay this ministry upon thy soul, but ye CAN make room in thy life for time apart with Me; and as ye place thyself at the disposal of the Holy Spirit, He shall use thee as a channel when the needs arise.

Nothing is more needful at this present hour than prayer power in full operation, under the direction and in the unction of the Holy Spirit.

I am calling My Spirit-filled believers to concerted and concentrated labor in this, the vineyard of prayer. Hidden from the eye of man, it is wide open to heaven; and the saints in heaven join with you in this operation of the love of God.

Other ministries ye must carry on yourselves alone, but in this ye have a mutual fellowship, for those in heaven have also an intercessory ministry for their brethren yet on earth.

Rejoice to be granted the privilege of so sacred a task. Count it most precious, and guard against the intrusion of distractions. Nothing is more important in My sight of all that ye can do for Me. Cherish it and cultivate it. Live in prayer, and ye shall know a full life of joy and the remuneration of My blessing!

A Yielded, Believing Vessel

Mine is the wisdom and the honor and the power and the glory and shall be so forever and ever. I make the nations to rise and I make the kingdoms to fall, but My throne shall be established in Zion and My righteousness throughout all the earth.

I am never in defeat, but I am held in abeyance at this present time by the selfishness and wilfulness of man. Yea, the going forth of My justice and of My mercy is obstructed by the ignorance of men and by the lack of faith in even My children.

Be not dismayed and ill of heart and spirit. Hast thou not read how I could not do mighty works in their midst because of unbelief? It is no less true today — and it is not in one place but in many places — yea, even throughout the length and breadth of the land.

Be aware of Me. I can accomplish great things through even one yielded, believing vessel. Remember David, and how I wrought a great victory for the armies of Israel through his courage, when all others were paralyzed by fear.

Move on, nor ever entertain the thought of retreat. Others may actually be going forward on the very path that would be for thee a retreat. They are not responsible to give Me the kind of service I ask of thee. Keep your eyes on Me, as I have counselled thee so many times before.

I have special expeditionary forces, and what if I have called thee to join these ranks? Don't look for the company of many others. Much of the way ye shall go entirely alone except for my presence.

Cherish My Words

O My children, obey My words. Do not wander in unbelief and darkness, but let the scripture shine as a light upon thy path. My Words shall be life unto thee, for My commandments are given for thy health and for any preservation. They will guard 'thee from folly, and guide thee away from danger.

Hide My commandments in thy heart, and make them the law of thy life. Cherish My words, and take not lightly the least of them. I have not given them to bind thee, but to bring thee into the life of greatest joy and truest liberty.

I have asked thee to give, in order that I may bless thee more. I have challenged thee to pray, so that I may respond and help thee. I have asked thee to rejoice, in order to keep thee from being swallowed up by anxieties. I have asked thee to be humble, to protect thee from the calamities that fall upon the proud. I have asked thee to forgive, so as to make thy heart fit to receive My forgiveness. I have asked thee not to love the world, for I would have thee loosed from unnecessary entanglements, and free to follow Me.

Sanctification is accomplished in no one by accident. Learn My rules, and put them into practice consistently, if ye desire to see progress in the growth of thy soul. Holiness is not a feeling — it is the end product of obedience. Purity is not a gift — it is the result of repentance, and a serious pursuit of God.

Comfort In Affliction

O My people, hath not My hand wrought for thee with many signs and wonders? Have I not ministered unto thee in miraculous fashion? How sayest thou therefore in thine heart, 'I will turn me again to the arm of flesh'? How oft have I spoken unto thee, and never failed to keep My word? Will ye not, then, trust Me now in this new emergency, even as ye have trusted Me in the past?

Thy need is deeper this time, and so I have made the testing more acute. I deepen you in the furnace of affliction, and purify your soul in the fires of pain.

Lean hard upon Me, for I bring thee through to new victories, and restoration shall follow what seemeth now to be a wind of destruction.

Hold fast to My hand, and rest in My love, for of this ye may be very certain: My love is unaltered; yea, I have thee in My own INTENSIVE CARE. My concern for thee is deeper now than when things are normal.

Draw upon the resources of My grace, and so shall ye be equipped to communicate peace and confidence to thy dear ones. Heaven rejoices when ye go through trials with a singing spirit. Thy Father's heart is cheered when ye endure the test and question not His mercy.

Be as a beacon light. His own glorious radiance shall shine forth through thee, and Christ Himself shall be revealed.

Return Unto Me

Return unto Me; for lo, I have sought after thee, but thou hast continued on in pursuit of thine own ways. I have called unto thee, but ye have disregarded Me. I have placed obstacles in thy path, hoping that ye would stop and consider and inquire of Me, but ye have obstinately and determinately forged on ahead.

Have ye learned no wisdom? Have past lessons fled thy mind? Are My dealings with thee remembered not at all?

O stubborn and rebellious child, has My love no longer the power to melt thy heart? Have My words which once ye so treasured become of no value to thee?

Put down thine anxieties, and trust Me for everything. Ye

need nothing but what I am fully able to supply, with no effort on thy part. I do not ask all My children to live in so complete a degree of trust, but I require it of THEE, because ye cannot please Me with anything less.

Ye are weary, and ye should be strong. Ye are encumbered, and I would have thee free. Ye are hindered by undue concerns, when ye should be abounding in joy.

Come back into My perfect will, and finish the task I have assigned thee, Anything else is sin. What, for another, may be legitimate is not so for thee.

Come close to Me, and I will minister to thee and will revive thy spirit. So shall ye go on, even though the climb be more steep than ever before.

One Day At a Time

O My child, hast thou known the way of the Lord, and canst thou trust Him now? Nothing shall befall thee but such as cometh from His hand. None shall set upon thee to hurt thee, for thy God hath built about thee a wall of fire.

Be content with what each day bringeth, rejoicing in thy God, for surely He it is who shall deliver thee and He it is who hath brought thee thither.

His way is discernable to the eye of faith. His heart is surely thy strong tower. In His affection thou hast security. In His love is thy hope and thy peace.

Do not question and do not doubt. Each day holdeth some small joy that shall escape thee if thou art preoccupied with tomorrow.

Nothing daunts thy Father. Nothing can restore the past and nothing can bind the future, but today thou mayest live in the full blessing of the Father's smile. Hold to His Words, for they are as a nail driven in a sure place. All else may seem shifting and non-permanent, but His Word is firm. It is a rock that shall not be moved. It is a firm place to stand.

Do not walk in the path of human reason, and resist the pressures that would project thee into conjectures of the future. Live one day at a time! Suffice it to keep thee occupied simply striving to bring joy to thy Father's heart. For ye know that He loveth thee, and ye shall find thy peace as thou resteth in Him.

The Blessings of the Pure in Heart

Lo, is not Mine heart drawn out toward thee to bless thee? Have I not said that I would shelter and protect thee and be thy strong support? Yield thy whole being to Me. I am thy loving Father. I know thine every need, yea, even before it ariseth. My provisions are not only sure, but full and overflowing, so that ye may confess with the Psalmist, 'I shall never want.' Ye shall see with a vision denied to many, for thy heart is pure, and to the pure of heart is the promise given that they shall see God. How much more glorious than to behold the beauty of a thousand sunsets! How much more thrilling than the sight of the fairest faces ever to grace this earth!

Yea, I shall reveal Myself to thee and ye shall know Me face to face, as Moses did of old. Ye shall walk with Me and shall talk with Me, and I shall hold thy right hand and shall be to thee as a brother and as a friend. I shall never leave thee, and in the darkness I shall be to thee a light. Yea, in joy I shall be an added comfort, and in sorrow I shall be to thee the peace that surpasses understanding.

Look not to man to tell thee more about Me. Look to Me directly, for I will reveal Myself to thee in a personal way and in ways of which no other could tell thee. I will be as personal and as dear to thee as I was to John, the Beloved. I would take thee aside as I did Peter, and talk to thee of things that concern thyself alone. I am not the God of congregations, but the God of the individual, and I am as concerned for thee as I was for Abraham or for Joseph or David.

Ye are never one of many to Me. Ye are precious and dear to My heart, yea, even as a very special treasure. For I love thee more than ye can ever comprehend, and I long to gather thee in Mine embrace and hold thee close to My heart. Do not hold Me at arm's length because ye have a sense of unworthiness. Have ye not read that the redeemed are brought near by the blood of Christ? Thy sins are not covered: they are washed away! They are not only forgiven: they are forgotten! Stay Me not.

Be as the prodigal when embraced by his father. Though he would have resisted for a moment, he swiftly accepted his father's forgiveness and reciprocated his love and affection.

I, too, would bring thee into My house and spread for thee a feast of blessings, and place upon thee the garment of praise, the ring of relationship and the sandals of peace. COME, for all things are prepared for thee and naught shall be denied.

The Healing Power of Joy

Say not within thyself, 'Lo, where is God?', for I say unto thee that I am within thee, yea, even in thine heart, and Mine hand is upon thee. Ye have looked in vain for Me because ye have sought to see Me in circumstances and in people, and have said, 'Lo, I find Him not.'

O My child, look to Me directly, and rest thine heart in Me. Do so with as little distraction as ye would find easy to do if you were the only human being in the world and therefore would have no one else to look upon and none else with whom to converse.

Praise Me. This I ask of thee in times when it seemeth indescribably difficult to do so. I ask it of thee in love that is stern at this point because I know unequivocally that it is your only hope for survival.

Distress of soul and grief of heart can only bring on destruction of body. Joy alone is a healer, and ye can have it in the darkest hour if ye will force thy soul to rise to Me in worship and adoration. I have not failed thee and ye have not failed Me. It is only that ye have failed thyself — or, so to speak, the disappointment has come on the human plane — not on the divine. Why should ye allow any human experience to alter or affect thy divine relationship with thy Father?

Bring thy sorrow, and watch for the sunrise of the resurrection. Yea, verily there cometh always a resurrection — a morning when hope is reborn, and life finds new beginning. Wait for it as tulip bulbs anticipate the spring. The rarest blooms are enhanced by the coldness of winter. The snow plays her part in producing the pageant of spring. But when the blossoms break through, we do not then turn back to thought of winter, but instead, we look ahead to the full joys of the coming summer.

So ye must do also. Thy God is thy maker. He is thy defender. And He is mighty to save. Yea, He is not only mighty to save from sin, but He is mighty to save from despair, from sorrow, from disappointment, from regret, from remorse, from self-castigation, and from the hot, blinding tears of rebellion against fateful circumstances. He can save thee from thyself, and He loveth thee when ye find it hard to love thyself.

Let His peace flow in thee like a river, carrying away all the poison of painful memories, and bringing to thee a fresh, clear stream of pure life and restoring thoughts.

This is not the end. Press on. The goal line is out ahead, and ye may yet be a winner in the race of life.

The Divine Commission

My child, do not chafe at the bit. It is I who have put it in thy mouth. I would have led thee by Mine eye, but ye have been wilful and stubborn. Ye question My direction because it is not the common way. But I would have thee take a path that is quite different from the paths of thy friends, and it is because I would bring thee into a place in Me and a ministry in which they have no part.

Do not hesitate, and do not falter. Move in and do so quickly, for I say unto thee, the hour is late, and there is great urgency because of the swiftness of the gathering darkness, yea, even the hour of which it is written that none shall be able freely to do My work. It is as when a great storm breaks suddenly and each person is fully bent upon finding his own personal place of safety. Even so it is coming to pass, that in this hour ye should be gripped with one consuming purpose — to find the place I have for thee.

I have deliberately put thorns in thy nest in order to drive thee forth. I understand thy reluctance, but I shall surely deal with thee until ye break out of thy bondage.

The enemy shall hinder thee in every way imaginable if ye give him any room to stand. Rebuke every detaining circumstance in My Name, and keep thyself covered by the blood.

Your heart will grow cold unless ye keep it close to Mine. Your love shall be turned to indifference unless ye keep the cross before thine eyes.

The Saviour loves the dying world and the lost sinner no less today than He loved them the day He hung on Calvary, bleeding and dying for their redemption. His grace is still as rich and His compassion is yet as deep. He has not become weary, nor has He turned His attention to other interests. The preaching of the Gospel is still His will, and the salvation of souls is His chief concern. So also should it be thine, and nothing else should be permitted to

28

take precedence over evangelism in thy life.

Be diligent. Confess thy lack, and repent of thy negligence. Then shall I give thee a fresh anointing and a new commission. Yea, I will give thee the tongue of an evangelist and will send thee forth to reap precious souls. Jesus, the Christ, shall be thy theme, and thou shalt uplift Him, and He shall draw the lost unto Himself.

Behold, the hour is upon thee. Look not back. Go straight forward, nor allow any to detain thee or turn thee aside. My purposes can only be fulfilled as ye give Me your undivided loyalty.

There has never been a day like this. Nothing of past experiences can be compared to it. It is as though in history there have been crests in the waves; but that which is ahead is like a tidal wave by comparison!

Sacrifice, My Status Symbol

O wicked and perverse generation: have I been so long in your midst and yet ye have perceived Me not? Have I not ministered unto thee in a myriad of ways, and ye have been blind? Yea, and when I speak unto thee, ye do not hear.

O My children, ye go your way as though ye belonged to another; yea, ye believe not as sons and daughters but as strangers. Ye hold meetings in My Name, and give honor to men, but not to Me. Ye boast that ye serve Me, but in truth ye serve your own ego; for that which ye do is calculated to enhance thine own position and advance thine own prestige, and ye give it all a sanctimonious cloak.

'See', ye say, 'we shall pray', while prayer is farthest from thy heart. And who shall hear thee? Only thine own ears. Prayer is for those whose hearts cry unto Me in sincerity, and who seek Me earnestly; not for those with only a pretended piety, and who, with selfish and unworthy motives and hearts made fat with self-adulation, are only playing with Me as a child would manipulate a puppet on a string!

Get you to the prayer closet! This is the reason I have taught thee to pray IN SECRET: because there ye are beset by fewer false motives and less temptation. He who does not habitually commune with Me alone is almost sure to find true prayer impossible in public.

Ye would make Christianity pleasant and acceptable: your Saviour did not find it so. You would make it comfortable and accommodating to your own schedule: He knew nothing of such a false religion.

Lonely nights, He wrestled in prayer, nor spared the flesh discomfort. Yea, and the more ye pamper the flesh as to bodily comfort, the more it shall demand of thee, until ye become its servant, and thy physical needs shall be a tyrant unto thee in thy house.

Be not deceived. I gave thee no such commandment. Hear Me as I repeat to you what I gave to your fathers: 'Deny thy SELF and TAKE UP THY CROSS, and FOLLOW ME.' Yea, follow ME — not some worldly form of a backslidden church.

Think not that it becometh blest because it bears the name church. My Church is a living body, not a dead form. My people may be recognized by their humility and sufferings; not by their social acceptability and their self-advertized success; not by extravagant physical appointments of their structures; but by the grace of God at work in their hearts. Sacrifice is My status symbol, and man has not been eager to decorate the type of spiritual leadership I had in servants like Paul and Jeremiah.

Do ye desire to follow Me truly? Look for the blood-stained prints of My feet. Go, as it were, to the cold, unyielding rock in the garden of Gethsemane, where self is put aside, and the cup of suffering is accepted. Die to thine own treacherous and deceitful heart. Rise with determination to go on unflinchingly, not hoping to spare thyself. Save thy life, and ye shall surely lose it. Offer it up to Me, this very day, in a renewal of consecration unto sacrificial living, and I will accept thee and thou shalt know joy as new wine.

Eternity And Time

Behold, a new day is dawning! Let not the sound of war and discord deafen thine ears to My message; for I would speak to thee a word of encouragement and would bring thee tidings of hope.

I say unto thee, My little children, I have not gone away never to return; but I shall surely come, yea, even at a time when ye feel the least expectation and when many shall have become engrossed in the problems of the hour.

Lo, I say unto thee, My beloved ones, do not become centered in the problems of the world; but look up, for surely your deliverance is near.

My ageless purposes are set in Eternity. Time is as a little wheel set within the big wheel of Eternity. The little wheel turneth swiftly and shall one day cease. The big wheel turneth not, but goeth straight forward. Time is thy responsibility — Eternity is Mine! Ye shall move into thy place in the big wheel when the little wheel is left behind. See that now ye redeem the time, making use of it for the purposes of My eternal kingdom, thus investing it with something of the quality of the big wheel. As ye do this, thy days shall not be part of that which turneth and dieth, but of that which goeth straight forward and becometh one with My great universe.

Fill thy days with light and love and testimony. Glorify and honor My Name. Praise and delight thyself in the Lord. So shall eternity inhabit thy heart and thou shalt deliver thy soul from the bondages of time.

Thou shalt experience a liberation from the pressures of time and shalt in thine own heart slow down the little wheel. So shall ye find a new kind of rest. Ye shall have a foretaste of the Sabbath rest, into which the whole earth shall enter before long. When this time comes, I Myself will slow down the little wheel of time, and there shall be an adjustment, and it shall be as it was in the beginning.

The pressures of time have increased as sin has increased, and all too often My children have been found living more in the little wheel than in the big. This happens whenever the flesh is in ascendancy to the Spirit. Whenever the opposite is true, ye have always experienced a fleeting but glorious freedom from the racing little wheel. Is it not true? Ye have found the Spirit always unhurried, and ye have marvelled to find how oblivious ye had been to the passage of time whenever ye have been truly in the Spirit.

Ye can live here as much as ye choose. Ye can enjoy this rest and disengage thyself from the little wheel as often and as long as ye desire. Ye shall lose nothing and gain much. Try it as a therapy for thy physical body. Always it shall most certainly be a tremendous source of energy and vitality for thy spiritual life!

LIVING WATER

And He said unto me . . . I am Alpha and Omega, the beginning and the end. I will give unto him that is athirst of the fountain of the water of life freely.

Revelation 21:6

Contents

He Hath Filled My Cup... 39

A Perpetual Fountain of Glory............................ 41

Ask! 42

Rivers of Living Water.. 44

Give Me a Drink.. 45

I Will Bring the Victory...................................... 46

Cleanse the Sanctuary.. 47

Ye Shall Not Be Earthbound............................... 48

Ye Cannot Weary My Love................................... 49

Courage 50

The Sense of Perspective...................................... 51

Remove the Rocks... 53

Put Away the Idols... 55

Saturate Thy Soul in the Oil of the Spirit........ 56

The Economy of the Kingdom............................. 57

Household Salvation 58

I Shall Gather My People.................................... 59

Check Thy Course.. 60

Set Thine Heart to Follow to the End............... 60

Break Loose the Fetters.. 62

A Garden of Fountains.. 63

An Instrument of Praise....................................... 64

He Hath Filled My Cup

Praise Him for His mighty works;
Praise Him for His marvellous grace.
Let all that is within me praise His wonderful Name.
Yea, let mine heart be lifted up in thanksgiving,
And let my soul rejoice with song.
For He hath delivered me out of the lion's mouth;
He hath lifted me out of the pit.
He hath put a song in my mouth;
He hath put gladness in my heart.
Yea, He is altogether lovely:
More than tongue can express or finite mind can know.
For He hath stretched forth His mighty hand
And hath smitten the waters:
He hath made me to pass through dry-shod. Hallelujah!
For there shall be no more sea. (Rev. 21:1)
There shall be no more any separation!
He hath removed every barrier; He hath bridged the gulf.
He hath drawn me unto Himself, yea, into Himself.
He hath left the enemy in confusion and defeat.
He hath led me through the way of the wilderness,
And His hand hath been a shade from the burning heat.
Through the barren wasteland, He hath filled my cup from living
streams.
He hath sustained, He hath delivered, He hath revealed Himself
In the cloud, in the fire, and in the Shekinah Glory.
Lo, as if this had not been enough,
He brought me to the banks of Jordan. There He did precede me:
For as the priests went first, bearing the ark,
So He did pass ahead in full possession of all His promises,
And thus He opened my way and
Brought me into the land that floweth with milk and honey.

(Josh. 3:16, 17 & 4:24)

A land of promise, a land of fulfillment;
A land of conquest, a land of victory.
A land of fulness, a land of abundance;
A land of fatness, a land of unreserved blessing.
Yea, He hath been unperturbed, though the inhabitants
Of the land be giants:
For in His sight they be as grasshoppers!
And one with Him shall be mightier than them all.
Yea, and He shall give me Hebron for an inheritance.
Let me not camp in the plain; but give me this mountain.
For though my youth was spent in the wilderness,
Let my strength be renewed:
Let mine eyes see with keener vision,
Let mine arm be mighty in battle. (Josh. 14:10-14)
For surely for this hour hast thou preserved my life.
As sheep Thou leddest us through the wilderness,
But now, O God, we stand in the Land;
As sheep no longer, nor Thou as Shepherd,
But Thou standest before us as the Mighty Captain of the Hosts
of the Almighty,
And we as men of war. (Josh. 5:13-15)
We seek no longer
To rest in green pastures and lie beside still waters;
For Thou hast issued Thy command to wipe out the giants,
And to utterly destroy the inhabitants of the land.
For Thy provisions are full and free and abundant;
But they are not uncontested.
Yea, the enemy seeketh by myriad means
To resist our every move toward conquest and possession.
Strengthen Thou Our Faith.
Make us mighty through God to the pulling down of strongholds.
Let us bind on the full armour of God
That we may be able to withstand the attacks of the adversary,
And that we may by the energy of Thy Holy Spirit
Deliver to him death blows. (Eph. 6:10-17)

Suffer us never to fall into his hands.
Fight Thou for us; and in Thy grace and mercy,
    Sustain us when we waver. Be ever close at our side,
And forbid that we leave the job unfinished as did Israel of old,
    And thereby suffer untold anguish.

For the Lord thy God bringeth thee into a good land, a land of brooks of water, of fountains and depths that spring out of valleys and hills. . . Deut. 8:7

A Perpetual Fountain of Glory

Write those things which I say unto thee. Write and hold back nothing of all that I shall say unto thee. For I shall speak unto thee in the darkness and shall make thy way a path of light. I will cry unto thee out of the confusion round about, and thou shalt hear My voice and shall know that which I do. For My way is hid from the rebellious and from the disobedient, and from them that seek to walk in their own wisdom.

But look thou unto Me, and I will be unto thee as a beacon in the night, and thou shalt not stumble over the hidden thing. Yea, thou shalt walk in a way of victory though turmoil be on either hand, even as Israel marched through the Red Sea on a path which My hand hewed out for them. Yea, it shall be a path of deliverance, and My Spirit shall go with thee and thou shalt carry the glad tidings of deliverance to a people that sit in darkness and captivity.

Tarry thou not for a convenient time, for lo, the movings of the Spirit are never convenient to the interests of the flesh; and I shall engineer thy circumstances to conform to My plan and My will, and thou shalt glorify Me; for My plan for thee excels all other ways, and in the center of My will there is a Perpetual Fountain of Glory.

Doubt not, neither hesitate, for I the Lord Thy God do go before thee, and thou hast already My promise that the work which I begin I am able to carry through to completion.

Yea, there is already laid up an exceeding weight of glory for those who go through with Me and determine to seize the prize. For I have wealth beyond thy fondest dreams to bestow upon them that have 'left all to follow', and all the glittering enticements of this transient life are as chaff in comparison, for the gifts and calling of God are without repentance, and My giving is restricted only by the will and choice of the recipient.

Lord Jesus, I cast myself at Thy feet. Yea, let me bathe them in tears, for lo, my feet have been as lead. Lo, they have been weighted down with the cares of this life. For I have been as one in a dream who seeketh to run and is held in paralysis.

Set me free, Omnipotent Lord, and make me Thy glad and willing bond slave. Loose my feet and make them swift to do thy bidding. Loose my tongue to shout Thy praise. Loose my heart to love the lost with the great deep compassion of Jesus Christ. Yea, free mine affections, and nail them to Thy cross! Amen.

Ask!

Behold, I have placed within thee a spring of living water. For My Spirit shall be a continual flowing forth of life from thine innermost being. This I have promised to all My children, and this ye may experience as ye claim it by faith. For all My promises are received by faith. None are gained by merit, nor are they awards for human achievements.

It is My Life that I am giving you. It is not an emotion; it is not a virtue, though these may follow subsequently. It is Myself. Divine grace, heavenly love, infinite mercy, fathomless peace, — all these shall spring forth unbeckoned and irrepressible out of the deeps within thee because My Spirit has taken residence there.

If there be dryness within thy soul and ye have not this life flowing forth, ye need not grieve, neither chide thyself for being empty. Fill up the empty place with praise. Thou mayest by praise open to Me the gates of the temple of thy soul. The King shall enter and bring His glory. The Rose of Sharon shall bloom in thy heart and His fragrance shall be shed abroad.

For the promise of the Father is to all who believe, yea, to all who are called, even those who are afar off. (Acts 2:39) And this promise is the gift of the indwelling presence of My Holy Spirit, promised to all who have been baptized in the name of Jesus Christ, who have repented of their sins and received remission. (Acts 2:38)

Yea, I say unto thee, it is a GIFT. Is it not written (Luke 11:13) 'how much more shall your Heavenly Father GIVE the Holy Spirit to them that ASK Him?' Ask, and ye shall receive, and your joy shall be full.

As surely as a door is opened in response to a knock; as surely as that which is lost is found by the one who searches after it; and as surely as one who makes a request receives that for which he has asked: even so, in similar fashion, and in a corresponding simplicity, I shall GIVE to you, My child, the Holy Spirit for no other reason than because you have asked Me to do so. I have not placed this blessing beyond your reach, for it is My desire that you shall have it.

How shall My Church be victorious without the dynamic power of the Holy Spirit filling each believer? Ye thwart My purposes and block My path when you do not avail yourself of this My provision. Do ye suppose I can accomplish My will through a powerless body? For each Christian is to be a channel through which My blessings may flow, and how can ye be so if filled with self? Only to the degree that ye allow My Spirit to flow in shall self be driven out.

The open heart shall be filled. The sin confessed shall be forgiven. The hunger after righteousness shall be satisfied. Be as a little child. I will be to you as a loving Father. You shall have what you desire because I love you. Let this be thy hope, and thy faith shall be rewarded. My power is not reserved for a few selected saints. It is available to all, and it is available to *you*. ASK!

Then shall the lame man leap like a hart, and the tongue of the dumb shall sing for joy; for waters shall break forth in the wilderness, and streams in the desert. And the burning sand and the mirage shall become a pool, and the thirsty ground springs of water. . . .

(Isa. 35:6, 7a—Amplified O. T.)

Rivers of Living Water

Behold, thou art in the hollow of Mine hand. Yea, in the moment that thou liftest thy voice to cry unto Me, and when thou raiseth thy voice to praise and magnify My Name, THEN shall My glory gather thee up. Yea, I will wrap thee in the garments of joy, and My presence shall be thy great reward.

Lift thine eyes to Mine. Thou shalt know of a surety that I love thee. Lift thy voice to Me in praise: so shall a fountain be opened within thee and thou shalt drink of its refreshing waters.

Pour out thy heart unto Me. From the deepest recesses of thy being, let thy love flow forth unto Me; let thy lips utter My Name.

Let thy praises rise in the daytime and in the night. Yea, when thou art utterly spent, then shall My speech fall upon thee. Then shalt thou lie down in peace and rise up in joy, and thou shalt be partaker of a perpetual fountain. As it is written: Out of thine innermost being shall *gush forth* RIVERS OF LIVING WATER.

Let the Word of God dwell in thee richly; for My Words, they are Spirit, and they are Life. They are living and powerful, and thou shalt wield them in faith effectively against the powers of darkness.

Behold, thou art in Mine embrace. REST THERE. For My Spirit and My ways are not to be mastered by intellect, but My love is to be received by those who long after Me and who reciprocate in kind. For so as faith receiveth the promises, and those who seek after eternal life are recipients of the faith of Jesus Christ (for faith is the *gift* of God) even so, they who long for a closer relationship with Me, to them shall I give a special portion of My love that they may have the power to love Me in return as I have loved them.

And I give not My Spirit and My love by measure. For I shall open My heart to thee and take thee within, even as in salvation thou didst open thy heart to Me that I might bring to thee eternal life. Yea, I shall hide thee in My heart that ye may experience constantly MY peace and MY joy. And thou shalt go no more in and out; but thou shalt dwell in Me as I have dwelt in you.

The poor and needy are seeking water when there is none; their tongue is parched with thirst. I, the Lord, will answer them; I, the God of Israel, will not forsake them. I will open rivers on the bare heights, and fountains in the midst of the valleys; I will make the wilderness a pool of water, and the dry land springs of water.

(Isa. 41:17, 18 Amplified O. T.)

Give Me a Drink

Behold, the time is short. Be not entangled in the things of the world, for they are transitory. Be not over-concerned as to thy personal needs, for your Heavenly Father knoweth what ye have need of, and He will supply. But let thine uppermost concern be to carry out My will and purpose for thy life, to be sensitive to My guidance, and to keep thine ear open toward Heaven.

Miss anything else, but don't miss My voice. Other voices may introduce disharmony, but My voice will always bring peace to thy heart and clarity to thy thinking. For ye shall hear My voice behind thee saying: This is the way, walk ye in it, when thou turnest to the left hand or to the right.

Yea, I will keep thee in the center of My will and My being, lest on the one hand ye move into coldness and doubt, or on the other hand ye be carried away by fleshly zeal. But there is no neutrality in the center. This is not an arbitrary position. For I will fill thee with the abundance of My own life.

Thy heart will burn with the Fire of My Love. Thou shalt rejoice in all kinds of circumstances, because I will share with thee My joy; and My joy is completely disassociated with the world and with the people of the world. But I joy in those who joy in Me. My love I pour out to those who pour out their lives to Me.

'Give and ye shall receive' is a spiritual law that holds true as much between thyself and God as between man and his fellowman. Even more so, for this is a higher plane of operation. Learn it on the highest plane, and it will become simple and automatic at the human level.

And even as I said to the woman at the well (knowing her need of true satisfaction) 'Give Me a drink', so I say to you, Give

45

Me a portion of the love ye have — even though it be limited and natural, and I will give you My love in return. Love that is Infinite. Love that is abounding. Love that will gush forth from thy life to refresh others.

Give Me just a cupful of your limited affection. I long for it. I weep for it as I wept for the love of Jerusalem. I will pour out upon you such love as ye have never known. Love that will flood your whole being with such satisfaction as ye never dreamed possible to experience except in Heaven. Lo, I beg of thee, 'Give Me a drink'. Or in the language of Elijah, 'Bake me a little cake FIRST', and thou wilt never lack for meal and oil.

(I Kings 17:13-16)

I Will Bring the Victory

O My child, have I ever failed thee? Have I ever turned My back upon thee, or forsaken thee? Have I not been thy refuge and thy strong defense?

I have protected thee and kept thee in sickness and in health. Yea, I am with thee to help thee now. Fear not. My purposes will be fulfilled in spite of thy weaknesses, if in thy need ye rely on My strength.

My will shall be done regardless of the flaws in thy life, if ye count upon the power of My righteousness. I do not work only in cases where there are no obstacles; but I glory in over-ruling the prevailing circumstances, and I take pleasure in bringing victories in those places where no victory is anywhere in sight.

Reckon upon My coming. Know that whenever faith brings Me on the scene, everything is changed. Darkness is turned to light. Grief is turned to joy. Sickness to health. Poverty to My sufficient supply. Doubt to faith. Anxiety to trust.

No negative force can occupy the same place as My Spirit. When My Spirit comes in, all these things must go. Yea, they *shall* go!

Ask for the victory. I will come and bring it. *Don't look for the victory* — *look for Me,* and ye shall see the victory that I shall bring with Me. After I have come, ye shall behold the miracles that I will do.

Cleanse the Sanctuary

Thus saith the Lord unto His people, come ye forth out of thy drowsiness. Yea, rise up and put on thy strength, O Zion; for the night is far spent. The day is at hand.

My people shall be a holy people, saith the Lord. But ye have gone in your own ways; ye have not considered it nor paused to take inventory. Return unto Me, and I will restore thee. Put away that which defileth and that which draweth away thine attention from Me, and I will walk again in thy midst as I walked in the midst of My people of old.

Yea, I will walk in thy midst in power and glory, and by My hand shall be wrought miracles. My power shall be manifested; My Name shall be glorified. For ye shall walk in newness of heart. With freshness of spirit shall ye serve Me; for I shall revive thee and bless thee, and pour out My Spirit upon thee, and thou shalt know that it is the Lord. He it is that healeth thee and forgiveth thy transgressions, that setteth thee upon a rock and establisheth thy ways.

With a WHOLE HEART have I commanded that ye love Me, and that ye serve Me with UNDIVIDED LOYALTY. Ye cannot serve two masters. Purge out, therefore, the old leaven, and make clean the vessels. CLEANSE THE SANCTUARY, and bring Me thy sacrifices with pure hearts and clean hands. The sacrifices of contrite hearts I shall not despise.

For I long after thee with a love that embraces Eternity. Though thou goest astray, I will surely draw thee back. Though thy love grow cold and thine heart indifferent, if thou shalt listen, thou shalt surely hear My voice. When thou turnest to Me, I shall bridge the gap. For though ye have strayed, I have not left thee. Wherever ye turn to Me in love and confession, lo, I am there in the midst of thee.

For My people have committed two evils; they have forsaken Me the fountain of living waters, and hewed them out cisterns, broken cisterns, that can hold no water. (Jer. 2:13)

47

Ye Shall Not Be Earthbound

O My children, what do you need today? Is it comfort; is it courage; is it healing; is it guidance? Lo, I say unto thee, that whatever it is that ye need, if ye will look to Me, I will supply.

I will be to thee what the sun is to the flower; what the water of the ocean is to the fish; and what the sky is to the birds. For I will be the giver to thee of life and light and strength. I will surround thee and preserve thee, so that in Me ye may live, move, and have your being, existing in Me when apart from Me ye would die. Yea, I will be to thee as the wide open skies, in that I will liberate thy spirit in such fashion that ye shall not be earthbound.

Ye shall live in a realm where the things of earth shall not be able to impede and obstruct and limit thy movement; but ye shall be freed in Me to a place where thy spirit may soar as the eagle, and ye may make your nest in a place of safety and solitude, unmolested and undefiled by the sordidness of the world.

Thou shalt have companionship; but it shall be the companionship of those like-minded with thee, yea, of those who like thyself have been done with the beggarly elements, and whose sense of value has been readjusted so that they deem the unseen as of greater value than the seen, and the spiritual riches more precious than the wealth of the world.

Be done with petty things. Be done with small dreams. Give Me all that you have and are; and I will share with you abundantly all that I have and all that I am.

Be to Me as a reservoir where I can store up My reserve of strength and power and blessing, and so make it readily available to the thirsty. Be never caught as the man in the biblical account who, having unexpected guests at midnight, had nothing to set before them. (Luke 11:6)

Take from Me largely, that ye be never holding an empty cup when the thirsty ask of thee a drink, and be never lacking when the sick ask for bread. (Mk. 7:27, 28) For if ye have but a little, I will multiply it; but if ye have not any, ye shall be ashamed.

48

Receive of My love freely. Drink of My Spirit — yea, drink deeply, so that it shall be truly 'waters to swim in'. (Ezek. 47:5) And move out by faith into the realms of the manifestations of My power, yea, mount up on the wings of My power. For there are powers of the air to be subdued and conquered. Thou needest faith and the liberty and power of the Holy Spirit to overcome these and to rise above.

For My Church Shall be an Overcoming Church, *and My Bride shall be a heavenly being.* I will not choose Me a wife out of Egypt. I will take to Me one who has chosen to make My home her home and My people her people, even as did Ruth. But she that turneth back shall be as Orpha, and even as Lot's wife. She shall not enter into My inheritance. Thus saith the Lord.

. . . whosoever drinketh of the water that I shall give him shall never thirst; but the water that I shall give him shall be in him a well of water springing up into everlasting life. (John 4:14)

Ye Cannot Weary My Love

Lift your eyes, and look upon Me. For though you have forgotten Me, I have not forgotten you. Whilst ye have busied yourselves with your daily occupations, *I have still been occupied with you.* When your mind has been captured by the affairs of life, *My thoughts have been of you.*

My little children, ye cannot weary My love. Ye may grieve My heart, but My love is changeless, infinite. I long for you to turn to Me. My hands are full of blessings that I desire to give you. I long to hear your voice. Ye speak much with others — oh, speak to Me! I have so much to tell thee.

I am not a remote power: I am an intimate person, even as thyself. Hast thou forgotten that I made thee in Mine own image and likeness? It is not that *I am as you, but you are like Me.* Do not let material and physical elements destroy your comprehension of Me as a *person.*

'Touch Me and handle Me', I said to Thomas. (Jno. 20:27) To thee I say: Cast yourself upon Me; pour your love out to Me. *You will discover that I am as tangible to thee as I was to Thomas.* Reach forth your hand, and lay it upon My broken heart. Yea, take hold of My nail-pierced hand. Now, can you still doubt My love?

Courage

My people shall not go mourning, for I the Lord shall be their rejoicing and their song. They shall not be a complaining people, for I shall take away the murmuring from your streets. Shall I lead into the battle fronts an army of weeping women? Shall I ask the faint-hearted to war?

Nay, but I shall give to My people brave and courageous spirits, and I will make them strong of heart. I will give them the spirit of the martyrs, for they shall be My witnesses of resurrection power. They shall be stalwart. They shall be stedfast. And I shall remove from the ranks those who are timid and those who desire comfort and security. My way is a way of sacrifice, and the rewards are not in worldly honors.

So take upon you the full armour of God: the helmet of salvation, the breastplate of righteousness, the loins girt with truth, feet shod with the preparation of the gospel of peace, having the shield of faith and the sword of the Spirit.

O yes, My people, this is a hand to hand combat. Ye shall stand against the foe face to face. Ye shall not turn in retreat lest ye be slain; for there is no armour to protect the back. The coward shall perish.

Ye have not wrestled in any measure such as He. (The Lord Jesus.) Ye are not prepared to enter into this conflict as long as ye are absorbed in the luxuries and the personal comforts of thy present life. For every soldier must give first place to his obligation to the armed forces, and second place to his own private life and wishes. Even so ye must do, if ye would be my followers. Even so did Jesus during His earthly ministry. His entire life was subordinated to the Father's will.

As it is written: 'Even Christ pleased not Himself.' (Ro. 15:3) How dare ye risk allowing the flesh to manifest its desires? They can be only evil continually. No good thing can come out of a deceitful heart. 'The arm of flesh will fail you — ye dare not trust your own.'

Only that which is generated within thee by the Spirit of God can bring forth righteousness; and be not conformed unto this world, but be becoming transformed by the renewing of your minds that ye may personally discover what is the good and acceptable and perfect will of God.

The Sense of Perspective

O My little ones, how precious you are to Me, saith the Lord — yea, as the apple of Mine eye, I shall guard thee from harm. Never let the fears that are common to the world creep into thy hearts, for ye are not of the world, My children, and ye need not fear the things that plague the minds of the ungodly.

Ye need not fear the coming judgment, for if thy sins have been confessed and forgiven and cleansed by the blood of Jesus, ye shall not come into condemnation, but ye are already passed from death into life. Ye need not fear the day of judgment. It is sent to try the world, and ye are not of the world, My little children. Indeed, it is you who shall help Me in judging the world.

Who know better than My children the crimes of the world? Have not many of them been perpetrated against you yourselves, even whilst ye sought to serve and worship Me? For mankind resisteth My hand upon them. But how can they punish *Me?* They can most naturally express their hostility toward the Almighty and show their resentment against My laws by ill-treating My children. Shall ye not be called to witness against them?

This is not incompatible with the law of forgiveness which now binds thee, for the scriptures say: Love thine enemies and treat with kindness them that do you wrong. It is the same with you as with Me. Today is the day of My grace, and it operateth through thee also, bringing loving forgiveness to all, even the spirit manifest by Jesus as He hung upon the cross. But the day of judgment shall be a day of strict reckoning, and it shall be a day of wrath against both sin and the sinner. It is inescapable, for it is appointed unto man once to die, and after this the judgment.

Do you fear calamity? Yea, ye are only human if ye do. But have ye considered My servant the apostle Paul? In shipwrecks, in adversities, in distresses, in physical privations, in persecutions and threat of death by wild beasts; in all of these, he rejoiced in his God. He was more than victorious. He was given a supernatural joy in the midst of all his distresses. Ye may have it too.

Have ye read the testimony of My servant, Habakkuk? And have ye read of the latter days of My servant, Job? There can be no permanent loss in the life of My children, for out of the seeds of every calamity riseth a whole crop of new victories. It is the way I have made it. The greatest evidence of this truth is Calvary. By design of man, out of the cruelty of wicked hearts, Christ was made a martyr. But by the Hand of a greater power, He was made to become the Saviour — even the Saviour of the very men who put Him to death.

No, My children, do not fear. Remember the words of holy scripture: 'Fear not, little flock, for it is the pleasure of your Father to give you the Kingdom'. Here you have it again — I am not simply preserving you, but I am doing so for the purpose of sharing with you My kingdom power. If ye can catch the vision of what the days ahead hold in store for thee in My great Kingdom, you will gain a whole new perspective, so that as ye view the present, transient scene, it will come into clear focus as to its true dimension in proportion to the whole panoramic picture.

I can give you the sense of perspective, because I see the whole scroll of the ages as it were already unrolled before Me — so that the future is as clearly in view as the past. Look over My shoulder! Look at your own life from My vantage point. My Spirit will bring thee revelation and understanding, light and wisdom.

The man of mature years has gained wisdom by experience. Ye may gain wisdom (if ye desire it) by, as it were, drawing on My experience. I am infinite and eternal, and though ye may be unable to grasp it, I have experienced both what is known to you as the past and what is referred to by you as the future.

You live within the confines of time. I live outside all such bounds and limitations. Selah!

Don't be disturbed by your ignorance. Seek diligently after My wisdom. It will greatly enrich thy life. Have I not commanded thee to do so?

It shall bring thee more tranquility than any other spiritual pursuit. It shall bring thee greater poise and sense of values than ye would ever be able to gain otherwise. For ye must profit either by your own experience or by My experience. What a contrast exists between the two!

Seek My wisdom, and make it the guide of thy life. Let the winds blow and storms beat. Thy house shall stand.

Remove the Rocks

O My people, I have called thee to repentance and confession and forgiveness and cleansing; but ye have listened to My words as though they were but slight rustlings in the tree-tops — as though they were of little consequence and could be brushed aside at will. Behold, I say unto thee: Ye cannot resist My Spirit without suffering pain; and ye cannot turn a deaf ear to My words without falling thereafter into the snare of the enemy.

Ye have not cried unto Me with all your hearts, but ye have complained that I have not heard your prayers. Lo, is it not written: 'The Lord is the rewarder of them that DILIGENTLY seek Him'? And again: *Then shall ye find Me, when ye seek for Me with ALL thy heart*.

Look no more to My hand to supply freely thy needs when ye have not humbled your hearts and cleansed your hands and come to Me with the sacrifice which I have required — even a broken and a contrite heart. Ye need not listen for Me to speak to thee when your ears are heavy from listening to evil reports.

Just as there can come no healing to the physical body until there be first a removal of the poison in the system: so there can come no blessing and revival and renewal to My Body, the Church, until there be a putting away of evil and a purging away of sins. Your eyes shall not look upon My face whilst they are still engaged in viewing the faults and imperfections in the brethren; and when ye look to Me in truth and sincerity and repentance, ye shall indeed see Me, and having seen Me, ye shall look upon thy brother with love and understanding and patience, knowing full well the needs in thine own heart and life.

Behold, after the weeds are cleared; after the fallow ground is broken up; yea, after the rocks have been removed: *Then will I send the showers,* and then will I minister to thy hearts in kindness and in blessing. For though My heart hath been grieved, yet I love thee; and though I have hid My face from thee for a time, lo, in great tenderness would I gather thee again unto Myself.

I will withhold My chastening rod when ye turn unto Me in repentance. If ye confess thy sins and recognize thy transgressions, I will be faithful to thee and forgive thee. I will cleanse and restore thee. Thou wilt find peace. Thou shalt say the tears of godly sorrow have been sweet.

The heart that grieveth over sin shall experience genuine comfort. There is not the like of it in any of the comforts of the world. If thou bathe My feet in thy tears, I shall clasp thee to My bosom in love. I cannot describe to thee My love. I can only give it to thee. It is beyond the Cross. Go through. The Spirit alone can communicate what lieth on the other side.

Put Away the Idols

Behold, I have put My Spirit upon thee that thou shouldest cry and not keep silence. Yea, I have spoken unto thee that thou mightest know the burden of the Lord, and that thou mightest understand what is in My heart.

For I love My people, yea, My chosen and elect; and Mine heart grieveth over them, because they are turned aside. They have known My love; yea, they have tasted of My goodness, and entered into My grace, and My salvation have I given unto them; but their love hath waxed cold, and their desires have been turned to others, and their ways are the paths of self-seeking and folly.

For I am a jealous God, saith Jehovah, and I will not share My glory with another. Yea, I will pour out My goodness without restraint upon every open heart; and to all who cry unto Me, I will be gracious.

BUT MY PEOPLE HAVE NOT CRIED: they have not called. Lo, they have been satisfied with the husks of this present world, and in an hour of indifference, they have allowed the pleasures of this life to fill that place which belongeth only unto Me. Yea, it hath displaced My Spirit, but it satisfieth not.

O that they might return unto Me, saith the Lord, for as the father waited the return of the prodigal, so long I for My people. Yea, Mine heart is lifted up with grief, and My tears flow as a fountain. For I love them: My soul is drawn out unto them.

Return unto Me, saith the Lord, and I will return unto you. PUT AWAY THE IDOLS, and give Me thy heart. Lay thine heart open before Me, and I will purge away the dross. I will cleanse it and fill it with My glory. Yea, thou shalt no more crave the leeks and the garlic of Egypt. Thou shalt no longer feed upon chaff; but I will satisfy thy soul with manna from heaven, and with milk and honey shalt thou be nourished.

And thy health shall return unto thee, and thy vigor, and thou shalt serve Me with fresh energy. Thou shalt go forth in new power, and My joy shall be thy constant portion. Though thou labor in the last hour before sunset, thou shalt be rewarded in kind like as those that preceded thee. (Matt. 20:1-16)

Saturate Thy Soul in the Oil of the Spirit

Through My people shall the eternal glory of the Father be manifested unto the nations. For the everlasting power of the Godhead is incarnate in My chosen ones. Is it not written that the kingdom of God dwelleth within you? In the day that ye make Me LORD in thy life and give to Me the sceptre and allow Me to reign within: then will I begin to move, and My power shall radiate forth from thine entire being. THEN will I bring to pass miracles — when ye walk in uprightness and with mercy toward thine acquaintances, and even toward thine enemies.

Do not imagine for a moment that I can do any mighty works in the atmosphere of hostility and evil and rebellion. Come unto Me with a cleansed heart and a right spirit: in sincerity, in honesty. If ye desire Me to work in thy midst, do not be devious in thy ways nor indirect in thy dealings with others. (II Cor. 4:2) It is the pure in heart who see God. It is those who seek after a holy walk and who set their heart toward holy living who inherit the promises and who come into My holy hill.

Know that in heaven nothing entereth that can taint nor mar. The beauty of the living God dwelleth there. Where there is holiness there is beauty: where there are beauty and holiness, there is omnipotence. Where there is the activity of the Almighty, there are forces of Life continually working to produce within thee a measure of the life and health and strength which are in Him.

Why will ye tolerate any idea of discouragement? Nothing can ever be accomplished for good in this frame of mind. Sin bringeth forth death; and any negative current flowing within thy body shall produce a steady regression.

I will prepare within thee a different attitude of mind. Thoughts that have been in confusion, I will reorganize. I will not bring to bear upon thee pressures that will cause thee to be weak. I will be to thee the strength which ye need. I will be to thee the inner fortification which will bear thee up even in the time of strain and crisis.

SATURATE THY SOUL IN THE OIL OF THE HOLY SPIRIT, *and keep thy channel of communication ever open to thy Heavenly Father.* His desire is toward thee, and He will be thy strong habitation.

The Economy of the Kingdom

Bring Me all the tithes, saith the Lord, and prove Me thus, if I will not open unto you the gates of heaven and pour down upon you a four-fold blessing. Yea, I will bless you in the grace of giving, and I will bless you with joy. Ye shall open the door of ministry for My servants, and ye shall partake of the fruits that shall come as a result.

Ye shall never give unto Me and become the poorer for it. Ye shall be given in exchange for thy small gifts My boundless riches, and through the contribution that cometh from a willing heart I shall be freed to bestow out of the abundance of heaven treasures ye could never with money purchase from the world.

But see that thy giving is with joyfulness — for God delighteth in a cheerful giver — otherwise thou grievest the Spirit, for has He not been given to thee without measure? Therefore, as ye have received freely (for God hath always a generous heart) even so it is required of thee that thou give without grudging, nor be mindful of any sacrifice.

Thy giving seems sacrificial only when viewed in the light of what other use ye could have made of the money. I say unto thee, give freely to the work of My Kingdom and I will add unto thee such other things as ye have need of.

Be My agents of righteousness and good will, and I shall prove Myself to thee as thy loving Heavenly Father, supplying thy needs out of the riches of My own treasury — and this, too, shall be to thee an exciting adventure in thy walk in the Spirit.

For ye shall see in what miraculous ways I will care for thy needs, and even in the process of doing this will further yet more the Kingdom; for others in giving to you shall receive spiritual blessings.

Yes, My child, My economy is wonderful! My Kingdom truly is not the kingdom of the world. Even thy material gifts when dedicated to Me become immediately "spiritual currency," and you have given to Me that which I can multiply to thee and to others in spiritual blessing.

Give, My children. Thy poverty shall be turned to wealth, and thou shalt be freed from thine anxieties concerning financial matters.

Household Salvation

O My child, I have loved thee with an everlasting love, and with strong cords have I bound thee to Me. In the day of adversity I have been thy refuge, and in the hour of need I have holden thee up, and thou hast found thy strength in Me. Thou hast seen My goodness on the right hand and on the left. Thou hast beheld My power, and My glory has not been hid from thee.

I have blessed thee out of the bounties of heaven and have not withheld from thee ought of what thy heart hath desired. Yea, and I would yet do more. For have I not promised that thou shouldest be saved AND thy household? And was not the blood applied to the lintel and the doorposts to the salvation of the entire family? (Ex. 12:22, 23)

So renew thine energies, and know that I am working with thee. For surely a light shall shine out of the darkness, and the faith thou hast exercised through the years shall be rewarded an hundred-fold. So thy faith shall be turned to sight; for thou shalt see with thine eyes and hear with thine ears and rejoice in thine heart over that thing which shall come to pass.

I will do a wonderful work, and thou shalt praise and glorify My name *together!* For He that keepeth thee neither slumbers nor sleeps. The Lord thy God is thy strength, and in Him is no weariness. He tireth not at thy coming, and thy cry is welcome to His ears however frequent.

Cast thyself upon His mercies; for His loving-kindness never faileth, and His grace and compassion are inexhaustible. His faithfulness is extended to all generations. (Isa. 59:21)

Lord God, thou art MY God; my hope is in Thee. Thou wilt never leave me nor forsake me. Thou wilt bring me through, and I will praise Thy Name!

I Shall Gather My People

Arise. Get thee up to the rim of the chasm, and look, and write what thou seest. For lo, death and destruction, darkness and thick mists, and the cries of them that perish shall rise, but there is none to hear. There is none to answer.

As it is written: Today is the day of salvation, and again: Seek ye the Lord while He may be found, for the night cometh. Yea, and My wrath shall be poured out upon the ungodly, and there shall be no hand stretched forth to save.

I have called in mercy, and in patience have I stretched forth Mine arm all day long to a careless and rebellious people. Yea, I have spoken from heaven, and My words have been set at nought. I have cried unto them through My prophets, and their hearts have been as molten stone.

They have lifted up their voices in defiance against Me, but there shall be none to deliver. There is no salvation in their hands, but they shall go down together. They shall perish together in their folly. For lo, the day of mercy is at an end, and the day of judgment is come.

Lift thine eyes to the clouds; for lo, the heavens are filled with glory. Yea, He cometh with ten thousand of His saints. Lift thine hearts, for thou shalt not be afraid because of those things which are coming to pass upon the earth. FOR I SHALL GATHER MY PEOPLE UNTO MYSELF; and in the hour of destruction, I will stretch forth Mine hand to deliver them. In the hour of wrath, I will snatch away My own — My Beloved — and the flames shall not touch them.

Surely My love is deep and abiding, constant and tender. I have not changed. For though nation rise against nation, and though war break forth into a universal holocaust; yea, though mankind in its folly dasheth itself to bits against the wall of the inevitable, yet have I not changed, saith the Lord God.

Mine heart is tender still. My thoughts toward thee are yet thoughts of loving-kindness. Yea, I look upon thee with a deeper love than ever before. As the bridegroom anticipating the approaching wedding maketh last-minute preparations and longeth for the hour of fulfillment; so doth My heart yearn for thee, My Bride, My Beloved.

Though thou see terror on every hand, only with thine eyes shalt thou behold and see the reward of wickedness. I shall preserve thee and keep thee, and thou shalt walk with Me in white.

Check Thy Course

There is never a day, there is never an hour, there is never a moment when you are outside My thought. As David said, 'Thou Lord thinkest on me'. Ye also can say this as surely as could David. Ye are no less dear to My heart, and I am equally concerned for you.

Go not into the path of folly, for My heart goeth with thee wheresoever thou goest; and I grieve over thee when thou art turned aside. Ye may not be going in the opposite direction. Ye may even be on a road that lies quite parallel with the one upon which I would have thee travel. But to be *almost* in the perfect will of God is to miss it completely.

CHECK THY COURSE. Chart it by My Word, and hold to it with rigid determination and be not led aside by the other little ships. For, as the scripture says: 'There were with them other little ships' — but Jesus was in only one.

Be sure you are in the boat with Him if ye hope to make it safe to shore in spite of the storms. For there shall be storms; but ye shall be safe if ye abide close with Me.

Set Thine Heart to Follow to the End

Show Me thy hand. Lo, I have fashioned it to bring glory to My Name. For My Name is above every Name, and unto Me belongeth praise and glory, and in Me shall every living thing rejoice. For I will cause a light to shine out of the darkness, and in that place where thou hast walked in defeat, there will I cause victory to break forth.

Rise, arise, and put on thy strength, O Zion; for thou art a people called by My Name, and in My Name shalt thou be strong and do exploits. And I will bless thee out of the abundance of heaven.

My strength shall be thy delivering power. For I the Lord am in the midst, to be to thee a mighty power, and there shall be none weak among you. But he that hath more abundant grace shall lend a lifting hand to him that hath less; and he that hath great rejoicing in his heart shall cheer them that languish.

For I know thy works. Thine heart hath been an open book which My Spirit hath read. Yea, and I know thine every desire, and I know thine every need, and I go before thee, and I shall bring it to pass.

In the morning, lift thine heart in song. In the evening, let thy requests be made known. And My peace shall keep thee, and My grace shall be thy support.

Turn not into the diverging path, neither fear to follow Me. For as the shepherd when he putteth forth his sheep goes before, so shalt thou know of a surety that I go before thee. And it shall be to thee a place of broad pastures, yea, of enlarged vision; of increased fruitfulness, and unbounded blessings — and nothing shall prevent Me.

Look not to thine own thoughts, but walk in the Spirit: so shalt thou accomplish the work which the Spirit desireth to do. Eternity alone shall reveal the fruit of this hidden ministry. For we labor not in the material realm, and we work not with the elements of this world; but our labor is in the realm of the Spirit, and the accomplishments are not judged by the human eye, but shall be revealed in the light of eternity.

Therefore be diligent. Follow Me so closely that there shall be no distance between. Listen carefully to My voice, that thou go not thine own way. For My path shineth more and more brightly unto that day. Set thine heart to follow to the end, for at the end there is laid up an exceeding weight of glory for them that endure.

Break Loose the Fetters

Behold, with a strong and mighty hand will I bring My people out. Yea, as I brought the children of Israel out from the bondage of Egypt and Pharoah, thus, and with a yet greater form of liberation will I bring My people out from under the yoke of Nicolaitanism and the shackles of legalism. *For My people shall be a free people, saith the Lord.* My people shall obey Me (not a human leader) saith the Lord. My people shall not labor in vain in the straw and stubble of the works of the flesh. But My people shall walk in newness of life and they shall be energized and led by My Spirit, saith the Lord.

Through the Red Seas, through the Wildernesses, through the Jordans, through the Promised Lands of spiritual conquest — I am with My people. *Let no fear dismay.* Let no aspect of the Past be a hindrance or stumbling block. For I bring you out of dead orthodoxy into Living Reality. I bring you out of traditions of the past into fresh revelations of Myself in this Present Hour.

The Past I use for thine instruction, but not as a blueprint of the present nor guidance for the future. Be not afraid to follow Me. Indeed, if ye but knew how close I am standing to the "curtain of time", ye would draw very near and be filled with expectancy. For one of these days — so very soon — the curtain shall be drawn; the heavens shall be rolled back; the canopy of the "sky" as ye know it shall be lifted away, and the Son of Man shall be revealed in power and great glory.

Then shall My Church be as a diadem upon My head; as tangible evidence of My kingship and victory. What manner of men ought ye to be with such a prospect in view!

BREAK LOOSE THE FETTER. Cast off the fears. Walk forth in Me in the conquering strength of My Holy Spirit.

A Garden of Fountains

Behold, My hand is upon thee to bless thee and to accomplish all My good purpose. For *this hour* I have prepared thy heart; and in My kindness I will not let thee fail.

Only relinquish *all things* into My hands; for I can work freely *only as ye release Me by complete committal* — both of thyself and others. Even as was written of old: *'Commit* thy way unto the Lord; trust also in Him; and He shall bring it to pass'. (Psa. 37:5) I will be thy sustaining strength; and My peace shall garrison thy mind. Only TRUST ME — that all I do is done in love.

For adversities must of necessity come. They are part of the pattern of life's pilgrimage for every individual; and who can escape them? But I say unto thee, that for those who walk in Me, and for those who are encircled by the intercessory prayers of My children, I shall make of the suffering, yea, I shall make of the trials a steppingstone to future blessing. (II Cor. 4:17, 18, Living Letters)

My arms are around thee, and never have I loved thee more! I will make thee like A GARDEN OF FOUNTAINS whose streams are fed by the mountain springs.

And the Lord shall guide thee continually, and satisfy thy soul in drought, and make fat thy bones: and thou shalt be like a watered garden, and like a spring of water, whose waters fail not. (Isa. 58:11)

An Instrument of Praise

O My child, I have chosen thee unto Myself, that I may make of thee an instrument of praise in My hand. I shall bring forth from thee a melody of praise and rejoicing, and cause the harp strings of thy soul to vibrate with a joyful song.

Bless Me with thy lips, and whisper My Name in adoration. I will free thee from the prison house, and thou shalt exalt thy God in liberty of spirit.

How hast thou said, 'I am insignificant and unworthy'? Lo, ye are precious to Me, saith the Lord, yea, even as the apple of Mine eye.

Turn not back in unbelief, but press onward and upward until the darkness is left behind, and ye shall come out into the light. Ye shall see Me then face to face, and know Me as a man knoweth his dearest friend.

Bring Me all that puzzles thee. Many questions need no answer, for when the heart is at one with the Father, there comes an illumination of Spirit which transcends thought. Understanding becomes a state of heart rather than an achievement of the mind.

Learn to worship, and thou shalt have rest of soul; yea, ye shall rise to a new place of fellowship, where ye shall be as the writer of the letter to the Ephesians said: 'seated with Christ in the heavenlies'.

Ye shall be taught of the Spirit; yea, He shall open to thee the mysteries of the Word; for it was by the Spirit of God that the Scriptures were given to holy men of old; even so, by the Spirit shall the treasures of the Word be revealed to thee.

In returning and rest shall ye be saved; in quietness and in confidence shall be your strength.

LAUNCH OUT!

"Casting down imaginations, and every high thing that exalteth itself against the knowledge of God, and bringing into captivity every thought to the obedience of Christ."

II Cor. 10:5

Contents

Launch Out! ....*Challenge* 71

I Will Put New Songs In Thy Mouth ....*Psalm* 72

From Center to Circumference ....*Encouragement* 72

Rain ....*Fellowship* 75

Shall I Commend You? ....*Humility* 77

My Energizing Power ....*Strength* 79

A Song At Midnight ....*Promise* 80

Keep Thy Face Toward The Sunrise ....*Comfort* 81

Your Body, A Living Sacrifice ....*Yieldness* 82

Conviction And Forgiveness ....*Forgiveness* 84

Look Not Back ....*Courage* 85

Fling Aside Thy Fears ....*Rest* 86

Run With Patience ....*Guidance* 88

Be Much With Me ....*Vigilance* 89

Be Not Afraid ....*Trust* 90

Seize Each Opportunity ....*Service* 90

The Art of Committal ....*Peace of Mind* 91

Whatsoever Ye Sow ....*Healing* 92

Chastening ....*Discipline* 94

The Last Great Outpouring ....*Revival* 95

Sing, My Children ....*Praise* 96

Launch Out!

Thus saith the Lord unto His people:
Lo, ye have touched only the fringes.
Yea, thou hast lingered upon the shore lines.
Launch out, yea, launch out upon the
vast bosom of My love and mercy, yea,
My mighty power and limitless resources.

For lo, if thou wouldst enter into all that I have for thee,
thou must walk by faith upon the waters.
Thou must relinquish forever thy doubts;
and thy thoughts of self-preservation thou must forever cast aside.
For I will carry thee, and I will sustain thee by My power
in the ways that I have chosen and prepared for thee.
Thou shalt not take even the first step in thine own strength.

For thou art not able in thyself —
even as flesh is ever unable to walk the way of the Spirit.
But Mine arm shall uphold thee,
and the power of My Spirit shall bear thee up.

Yea, thou shalt walk upon the waves,
and the storm shall but drive thee more quickly to the desired port.

Chart and compass shalt thou not need,
for lo, My Spirit shall direct thy goings,
and are not the winds held in My fist?

Be not fearful but believing.

I Will Put New Songs In Thy Mouth

O my soul, wait thou upon God, and He will do thee good.
  Yea, He will be to thee refreshing to thy soul.
For His tender mercies are never-failing,
    and His kindness toward thee is as the morning.
As the sun riseth with healing in his wings,
    so shall thy God be unto thee.

For the night is past; yea, I bring thee into a new place: a place
of rejoicing in Me such as ye have not known as yet.
For I shall fill thy soul with fatness, and I will be with thee
  to do thee good. I will make thy hands to war,
    and I will make thy lips to praise Me with songs.

I will put new songs in thy mouth, and thou shalt
rejoice in the Lord thy God for He is a Mighty God.
    He delivereth, and no man can bind:
    He lifteth up and none can pull down.
Yea, He doeth valiantly, and who can prevent Him?

From Center to Circumference

Lo, thou seekest revival.
Thou doest well; only seek it not in the energy of the flesh.
  For the flesh is ever intent upon its own interests;
      yea, it ever lusteth after those things
          which do perish with the using.
  For I would that ye might seek Me in Spirit:
      then would I come down upon you in all My fulness, and
would hold back nothing of all that I desire to do unto thee.

For My ways are hid from them that
seek Me in the energy of the flesh.
Deep calleth unto deep at the noise of the waterspouts, (Psa.
42:7) and lo, *I am in thee,* yea *for this very purpose* above all
other purposes, have I taken up Mine abode WITHIN thee; that
My Spirit might be diffused through thy spirit, and that we might
be one even as I am one with the Father.
I in thee, and thou in Me,
that we might be unified in thought and in action:
in devotion and in purpose,
that we might move continually not as two, but as ONE.

I ask thee not to DO, but to BE.
For whatsoever is of the flesh is flesh;
but when thou shalt allow My Spirit to have *free course,* when
thou dost cease to interfere with My moving within thee,
then those things which shall be accomplished
both *within* thee and *through* thee
shall be verily the LIFE OF GOD.
For My Spirit is the Spirit of Life,
and My Spirit is the motivating power of Divine energy.
ALL ELSE IS DEATH. As it is written,
"Flesh and blood CANNOT inherit the Kingdom of God."
Neither can man through any endeavor of his own,
however holy his purpose,
produce this life, which does not exist
apart from the direct activity of the Spirit of God.

For I am WITH you and I am IN you
to make thee neither barren nor unfruitful.
I am IN THEE to give thee Life,
and to give it to thee ABUNDANTLY,
yea, LIFE WITHOUT LIMIT.
For all I am able to do for thee is limited only by My
omnipotence and My eternal, everlasting Life and Power,
and to these THERE ARE NO LIMITS!

Lo, I wait to bless thee;
I wait to give thee of My fulness.
I delight to do for thee
for I love thee beyond thy power to begin to know.
Only drop those things which thou graspeth in thy hand,
and place thy hands in Mine.
Only wrest thine eyes from those things thou holdest precious,
and I will fill them with My glory.
Loose thine affections from all others.
Place in My hands those thou holdest dear.
Leave them in My keeping:
for so shall thy heart be set free to seek Me
without distraction.
For when I am become to thee more precious than all beside;
when I am become to thee more real than all else;
and when thou lovest Me more than thou lovest any other,
then shalt thou know *complete satisfaction*.

Thy peace shall flow as a river,
and thy joy shall overflow as a fountain,
and My glory shall be poured out as the fragrant anointing oil
upon all thine other relationships.

For I purpose NOT to strip thee of earthly ties and joys,
but I long to have thee give to Me the center of thy life
that My blessing may flow out to the circumference.
For My Spirit moveth not from the circumference to the center,
but from the *center* to the *circumference*.

So yield to Me thy very inmost consciousness.
Offer Me not some random portion of thine affections,
but give to Me that deepest portion of thy heart,
yea, that which seemeth to be thy very life itself.
For in very truth it is so.
For thou yieldest Me thy life only as thou profferest thy love.
For this reason have I said, love is the fulfillment of the law.
So give Me WHOLLY thy heart's affections
and I will meet thine every need.

Seek ye FIRST the Kingdom of Heaven;
set your desires wholly to obtain the riches of God,
and all other things shall be freely supplied
 according as the needs arise.

Only be thou very diligent in the quest,
for the enemy is ever laying wait
that he may through evil device turn thee aside.
 Be not overtaken by his wiles.
 Set thy face as a flint.
Lay aside every weight and deliberately remove every hindrance.
 Give thyself unto prayer.
Thou hast My word, yea, thou hast My promise,
 that they who seek shall FIND.
And My promises are yea and amen,
 and My Word shall never pass away.

Rain

O My child, I love thee, I love thee.
Get thee to the hills and look, for lo, there cometh rain.
The drought is over and past, and the sound of rain approacheth!
 Yea, I will send showers of blessing
 upon the hearts of my waiting people;
for before they call, I have prepared to answer,
and while they are seeking Me,
 I shall come down upon them.

 O Lord, tarry not. We wait for Thee.
 We long for Thee. Yea, our souls pant for Thee
 as the thirsting deer panteth for the waterbrooks.
 For we desire Thee with an unrelinquishing desire;
 yea, we cannot be denied, for *there is no alternative.*

O My child, I love thee, I love thee.
Lift thine eyes to the heavens, for lo, they are filled with
clouds; yea, they are heavy with water.
Get thee back to the camp.
Set out the buckets and make preparation:
for already the wind rises, the leaves rustle in the trees;
the birds hasten to their nests, and lo, I come.
I come to revive and to refresh.
I come to quicken and to cleanse.
I come as floods upon parched ground.
So shall new life spring forth,
and the desert shall be filled with flowers.
For since time was, have I never forsaken My people.
I have undertaken for them; I have protected them.
I have delivered them in every time of need.
I have rescued them from every calamity;
I have denied them nothing of the desires of their hearts.
They have not always asked in wisdom,
but I have never failed to respond. *(Psa. 106:15)*
Think ye I love My Church less than I loved ancient Israel?
Think ye I stretched forth Mine hand for them,
and through mighty miracles set them free from the bondage of
Pharaoh, and made them a way to escape through the Red Sea,
and provided for their daily needs through the wilderness jour-
ney, and gave them water out of the Rock,
and will do any less for THEE?

For thou art twice-beloved.
Thou art My body, the Church, and thou art My Chosen Bride.
Yea, thy slightest wish is My command.
For I delight to please thee,
even as a bridegroom seeketh to please his bride.
How much MORE do I long to bestow upon Thee tokens of My
affection? And My love for thee surpasses all human
comprehension.
For I am not a man that I should be limited;
and I need not divide My Spirit among many,
but I long to share with EACH My fulness;
and there is no partiality in My love.

Look not upon thy lack of capacity, for I shall enlarge thy heart.
Open not thy mouth to question Me,
for love questioneth not, but receiveth gladly and freely.
Do thou even so, and thou shalt not be disappointed.
Be not dismayed,
neither give heed to thy sense of unworthiness,
for lo, I have loved thee *simply because I have loved thee,*
and what need I of any other reason?
Dost thou not thyself do likewise in human relations?
Shall I not shed My love upon thee for no other reason
than simply that I have CHOSEN so to do?
Otherwise were it not love in its purest sense.

For only as thou knowest with certainty
that I love thee *though thou bring no gift,*
can ye return to Me love that will remain constant
both when I bless, and when I withhold.

———————

Lo, Thou art mine. Thou hast dove's eyes.
Kiss me with the kisses of Thy lips,
for Thy lips are sweeter than honey.
Gather me in Thine embrace,
for Thine arms are stronger than the bands of Orion.
All eternity is held in one moment in Thy presence,
and all of time is vanity apart from Thy fellowship.

Shall I Commend You?

Behold, I say unto thee: Is it a small thing that thou shouldst weary the Lord God Almighty with thy complaints?

Is it a light thing in Mine eyes that ye walk in weakness when I have made full provision that ye might appropriate My strength?

Have ye not wrought insult to Me in that I have condescended to dwell within you, and ye have set Me aside, and quenched and grieved My Holy Spirit and walked in your own ways?

Shall I commend you?
Shall ye escape My rebuke and displeasure?
Thou lookest in vain for My smile.
For thou thinkest in thine heart
that thou canst bring Me some gift.

'I will do Him a kindness', thou hast said, and hast thought I
would accept this as devotion.
Be not deceived. God is not thus to be trifled with.
'See', thou hast crooned, 'I have brought thee this basket of fruit'.
Cursed be the ground that brought it forth!
Have I not required *blood?* But thou hast loathed sacrifice.
But I have said, I will have none of your pretty gifts,
for God desireth integrity, and behold, to obey is better than all
thine vain attempts to appease.

Behold, I am angry with you, and not without cause.
Thou hast profaned My sanctuary with vain endeavors in the flesh.
Thou comest not to Me in spirit and in truth; but thou hast
set limits of thine own making to check Me and hinder Me.
Thou sayest thou fearest to offend;
but I say unto thee, for the very hardness and wilfulness of thine
own hearts, thou wilt not yield Me control.
Thou keepest it in thine own hands lest
thine iniquities be uncovered and thy shame appear unto all.

Lo, I will have none of it.
I will come unto thee when thou hast humbled thyself.
I will purge thy sins when thou puttest away thy sham and
hypocrisy.
I will gather thee to My heart when thou shalt cease loving thine
own selves.

The days are short.
Will ye that I come unto thee with a rod or in love?

My Energizing Power

O My child, I have waited long for thy coming.
　　Mine eyes have grown weary in watching,
　and Mine heart heavy with longing after thee.
For I have said 'Rest in Me', but ye have striven.
I have said 'Stand still', but thou hast continued to run.
I have called, but ye have been listening to the voices of men.

　　　Lo, I say unto thee, Turn unto Me.
Thou needest do no more. For thou wilt find thy quest ended.
Thou wilt see then how futile has been all the struggle.
For like the sinner who misses the gift of saving grace through
　　　　　absorption in good works,
　　　so thou, My child, hast missed My sweet reality
　　　in thy frantic effort to please Me.

As Martha in her desire to minister to Me forfeited My nearness,
　　so thou hast done.
My child, I have need of nothing. I desire only thy love.
Give Me this first always, and whatsoever service may follow,
　　thou wilt then do with light feet and a heart set free.
　　　Abandon to Me thy whole being,
　　and I will then work in and through thee in such a way
　　　that even as I am using thee,
　　thou shalt simultaneously experience My energizing power;
so that in the very process of giving, thou shalt in very truth
　　　receive even beyond what ye give,
and shall in each instance emerge richer and stronger.

　　　There is no loss when ye serve Me thus.
For when thy life is wholly lost in My life, there is never anything
　　　　　　　　　but gain.
　　　As the prophet of old exclaimed,
　　　'They go from strength to strength'. *(Psa. 84:7)*
Only sin worketh death and loss. Righteousness worketh life and
　　　　　　　　　health.

So come first to Me.
Yea, come until the stream of thy life
is swallowed up in the ocean of My fulness.
Then shalt thou go, and thou shalt give,
and in thy giving thou shalt never know lack.
The Lord is thy shepherd; thou shalt not want.
For the kingdom of God is righteousness and peace and joy in
the Holy Ghost. *(Ro. 14:17)*

A Song at Midnight

Behold, I am near at hand to bless thee,
and I will verily give to thee out of the abundance of heaven.

For My heart is open to thy cry; yea,
when thou criest unto Me in the night seasons,
I am alert to thy call, and when thou searchest after Me,
the darkness shall not hide My face,
for it shall be as the stars which shine more brightly in the
deep of night.

Even so shall it be. And in the night of spiritual battle,
there shall I give unto thee fresh revelations of Myself,
and thou shalt see Me more clearly
than thou couldst in the sunlight of ease and pleasure.
Man by nature chooseth the day and shunneth the night;
but I say unto thee
that I shall make thy midnight a time of great rejoicing,
and I will fill the dark hour with songs of praise.

Yea, with David, thou shalt rise at midnight to sing.
It has been written, 'Joy cometh in the morning',
but I will make thy song to break out in the night.
For he who lifts the shout of faith and praise *in the night*,
to him verily there SHALL be joy in the morning.

Keep Thy Face Toward the Sunrise

Behold, I have sent thee out alone,
    but I have gone before to prepare thy way;
yea, through the darkness to bear a light.
    I ask thee only to follow Me,
for I will surely lead thee in a safe path
    though dangers lurk on every hand.
    Yea, I will be thy protection:
      I will be thy comfort.
        I will be thy joy.
I will turn the bitter tear to sweet perfume.
    By My Spirit, I will mend the broken heart.
I will pour warm, fragrant oil into the deep wound.
    For Mine heart is fused with thy heart,
      and in thy grief, I am one with thee.
        Yea, I will fill the vacant place.
Mine arms shall hold thee, and thou shalt not fall.
My grace shall sustain thee, and thou shalt not faint.
    My joy shall fortify thy spirit
even as a broken body is rejuvenated by a blood transfusion.
    My smile shall dispel the shadows,
      and My voice shall speak courage.
Yea, I will surely keep thee, and thou shalt not know fear.
Thou shalt rest thy foot upon the threshold of heaven.
    I shall hide thee in My pavilion.
    Thou shalt have My constant care.
    I will not leave thee for a moment.
    I will keep thee from despair:
    I will deliver thee from confusion.
    When thou art perplexed,
I will guide thee in wisdom and in judgment.
By thy light shall others be led out of the valley.
By thy courage shall the weak be lifted up.

By thy steadfastness shall he that wavereth be stabilized.

Lo, the hour is upon thee.

Look not back.

Keep thy face toward the sunrise,

for He shall rise fresh daily in thy soul

with healing in His wings.

———————

Under every burden, God will slip His hand —

Every gulf of sorrow, His great love has spanned.

Into every heart-ache, God will pour His balm;

Ease the pain and anguish, bring a blessed calm.

Your Body, A Living Sacrifice

Behold, I say unto thee: Yield Me your body as a
living sacrifice, and be not conformed to the things of the world,
but be ye transformed by the renewal of your mind.

Set your affections on things of the Spirit,
and be not in bondage to the desires of the flesh.

For I have purchased you at great price.

Yea, thou art My very special possession and My treasure.

I would have thee to set thine affections and desires upon Me
even as I have set Mine heart upon thee.

It is written that the wife hath no power over her own body except
for the husband, nor the husband but for the wife. (I Cor. 7:4)

So I would that ye should yield your body to Me, otherwise I am
limited in My power to work.

For I must have a vessel through which to operate.
I would have you to be a vessel not only yielded to Me, but puri-
fied, dedicated, sanctified for My use; available to Me at all
times, and ready to be used at whatever time I have
need of thee.
Thou wilt not have time to make thyself ready when I need thee.
Thou must be already prepared.
Thou must keep thyself in a state of readiness.
Thou canst not live to the flesh and at the same time be available
to the Spirit.
Ye must walk in the Spirit, and in so doing
keep thyself from becoming entangled in the things of the flesh.
Ye must live in obedience to the Spirit,
and thus be kept from being in bondage to the desires of the flesh.
I Myself cannot keep you except ye first make this choice.
It was concerning this matter that Jude wrote his word of ad-
monition: And ye, beloved, building yourselves up in your most
holy faith by praying in the Holy Ghost, keep yourselves in the
love of God. *(Jude 20, 21)*
By setting your soul *through deliberate choice of your will*
to pursue the worship of God by praying in the Spirit,
thou shalt find thy faith strengthened
and thy life bathed in the love of God.
With thy faith laying hold upon God's promises and power,
and thine actions motivated by the love of God,
thou wilt find thyself in the path of the *activity of God:*
His blessing shall be upon thee,
and He will accomplish His works through thee.

Thou needest make no plans nor resort to any clever strategy.
Keep yourself in the love of God.
Pray in the Spirit. Rejoice evermore. Set your affections upon
Christ.
God will do through you and for His glory such
things as it pleases Him to do, and thou shalt rejoice with Him.
For as thine own spirit is aware when His Spirit is grieved within
thee, so shalt thou also be aware when His Spirit *rejoices*
within thee. This is His joy. This is the joy He promised.

This is the greatest joy that can come to the human heart, for it is the joy of God, and the joy of God transcends the joy of man.
Surely thou shalt not only rejoice but be exceeding glad, with a gladness surpassing thy power to tell.
So shalt thou give this back to Him,
since no other can fully receive it,
even as David poured out to Him
the precious water from the well of Bethlehem.

(II Sam. 23:15, 16)

Praise His wonderful Name!

Conviction and Forgiveness

My patience is running to an end, saith the Lord. For I have purposed and man hath despised. I have planned, and man hath set at naught. I have willed and ye have resisted Me. Be not smug in your own ways; for your ways are not My ways, saith the Lord.

Ye are indulgent when I have called you to rigid discipline. Ye speak soft words when I would require of thee to speak the truth. Ye interfere with the convicting work of My Holy Spirit when ye smooth over confession. I am not a severe God, unmindful of the frailties of human nature, but I am a God of divine love and holiness, and I desire your fellowship, and I long for you to know the joy of Mine.

Man cannot forgive sin. Why do ye then excuse either thyself or thy brother? Before Me ye stand or fall. Confess your faults one to another, and pray for one another that ye may be perfected. Rebuke, warn, and exhort each other with all longsuffering and patience. Love and forgive each other, but do not lighten conviction.

My love and My holiness are beyond your comprehension. I do not love you because you are sinless (how then could I love any?) but I am able to receive you into My fellowship and bring you close to My heart on the merits of the shed blood of the Lord Jesus Christ. Here only rests your hope of cleansing and accept-

84

ance. Here is the only door of access between sinful man and
a holy God. But here indeed is all that ye need.

Then why set about to excuse and rationalize your sins
when the way of confession and forgiveness stands open to you?
Hinder Me not for time is precious, and I am waiting for thee.

Look Not Back

Behold, in the hollow of My hand, there have I made thee a nest,
    and thou shalt lay thee down and sleep.
        Though the elements rage,
        though the winds blow and the floods come,
            thou shalt rest in peace.
For, O My child, thou art precious in My sight.
I know thee by name, for thou art not the child of a stranger,
    but the fruit of Mine own loins. Yea, I have begotten
thee, I have called thee by thy name, and thou art Mine.

Be not dismayed, for as I suffered,
        so shall ye suffer in the world.
    I have not taken thee out of the world, but I am with
thee to help thee and to encourage thee, and to give thee
strength in all thou shalt be called upon to endure.

        Thou facest each new day with Me at thy side.
        (Never forget that I am there.)
        Thou meetest every difficult circumstance
            with Mine arm outstretched to fight for thee.

Lift not thine hand to attempt to accomplish any slightest task
        in thine own strength. This have I forbidden.
God helps not those who help themselves,
        but He is the champion of those who cannot help themselves,
        and of those who are wise enough not to try.
It is not thy cooperation for which I have asked,
        but thy submission.
            Not that thou go alone until thou fallest,
        but that thou draw upon My strength for *every step*—
    both the smooth and the rough.

If thou form the habit of trusting Me in the easy way,
thou shalt find it the natural thing to lean upon Me
in the difficult situation.
And if I bring thee through the river in summer,
thou shalt not fear to trust Me in flood-time.

So clasp thy hand in Mine, and loose not thine hold.
For thou canst not tell what great thing I may do for thee
through some smallest happening.
Thine every hair is numbered,
and the most incidental occurrences of the most ordinary day
I delight to choose and use to reveal to thee
My earnestness in helping thee.

Clasp Me to thine heart,
for I love thee with an everlasting love,
and with strong cords have I bound thee.

Look not back, but look ahead,
for I have glory prepared for thee.
Yea, when thou lookest on My face
thou wilt surely say that these present sufferings
are in no way comparable
to the glory which I have in store for thee.

Fling Aside Thy Fears

Lo, I have sought thee,
following thee upon the hills and pursuing thee through the
barren wastes.
Yea, I have called after thee, but thou hast not heard.
Thou thoughtest in thine heart that thou wouldst find Me,
and thou hast set out in thine haste to seek for Me,
but thou hast looked for Me in vain.

Thou hast scanned the horizon from day to day,
until thine eyes fail thee from thy searching,
as the traveler seeking in vain for a spring in the desert,
and finding none languisheth for water and fainteth in the heat.

Lo, as Hagar of old, thy tears have blinded thine eyes whilst meantime I have revealed My glory and made My provisions apparent to the child. (Gen. 21:17)

For it is written, 'Except thou become as a little child,
ye shall in no wise enter in.' (Lk. 18:17)

For My ways are hid to those who seek Me in impatience,
and the eyes which seek Me in human wisdom shall never find Me.

For I am found of them that seek Me
in utter simplicity and in candid honesty.
Rebuke Me not,
neither complain that I have left thee alone.

Lo, I am at thy side, but thy fretfulness
has raised an iron curtain between.

For when thou art utterly finished
and exhausted in thy struggling;
when thou hast come to an end in all thy striving;
when thou art ready to desert thine intellectual pursuit,
and when thou shalt cast thyself upon Me
as a babe upon its mother's breast;
then shalt thou know surely that I have been constantly
at thy very side; that I have never deserted thee.

Yea, that My love for thee is of such nature and intensity that it would be impossible that thou couldst ever escape My thoughts, or that My longing after thee could ever waver.

Cast aside thy questionings.
Fling aside thy fears.
For surely Mine arms are already outstretched to receive thee:
Only believe.

For in the moment that thou relinquish *all*—
in that same moment shalt thou know release.

For thou shalt be set free of thyself
and thou shalt be captive of My love.

Mine arms shall gather thee, and I shall never let thee go!

87

Run With Patience

O My child, there is nothing that I would hold back from thee.
If thou wilt heed My Word, if thou wilt listen to My voice,
   I will surely lead thee in a plain path.

Set thine affections upon Me and keep them there.
     Center thine attention upon me.
Yea, set thine heart to follow after Me with singleness of mind.
   This will remove all doubt at every crossroad.
   This will keep thee continually at My disposal.
     Never set out upon a "project".
     My Life is not project but overflow.

Thou hast already witnessed the verdure of life that has sprung
forth where the waters of My Spirit have flowed.
     How can any doubt remain?
     But the flesh dies hard; it is true.
Even Jesus learned obedience through suffering and self-discipline.
And Paul admonished: 'Endure hardness as a good soldier.'
     All that comforts the flesh weakens the Spirit.

I could by adversity strip from thee the comforts of life,
     but I will bless thee in double portion,
if of thine own accord ye do as Paul and lay aside every weight,
and resist the divers temptations that continually beset thee
   and run with patience the course as I set it before thee.
     "Running" with "patience".—
In these two words I have combined the intensity of purpose and
the quiet waiting upon Me which ye needs must have, else ye
be overtaken in the race by fatigue of body and soul.

     So as I have told thee before,
Come to Me and pour out thy praise and thy love and thy worship.
I will bless thee and guide thee and use thee in My own good
time and pleasure.
     Thou shalt not be disappointed.

Be Much With Me

For My people, saith the Lord, set the watch in the night-time; yea, rise and pray, and let not that hour come upon thee unaware.

For the time is short, yea, the storm is gathering fast. Ye see clouds in the sky, and ye say rain is approaching.

Can ye not discern the events that are currently shaping up in the affairs of men, and be as keen to observe their import and know that disaster and holocaust are in the making?

But thou art prone to fall into the same snare as others — to presume that prosperity and peace will continue, simply because ye wish so strongly that it might be so. Ye are not ignorant concerning the prophecies of My Word as some are, and yet ye allow the feelings and attitudes that are abroad in the land to invade your own personal life.

Be more with Me, and let My Spirit pervade thy spirit, and then thou shalt be more influenced by Me than by the world around you. But be prepared for the fact that ye will then be of a different mind and attitude than those around you, and be willing to accept the difference and be able to ignore misunderstanding.

For many will not accept a message of warning, because they have set their own personal ambitions against the will of God, and they are so intent upon their own pursuits that they refuse to tolerate the thought of possible interference of any kind.

But you, beloved, be much with Me, for there is a great and heavy burden on My heart. For God taketh no pleasure in the death of the wicked. My long-suffering and grace have continued because I deeply desire that all men should come to repentance. But the grapes of wickedness are full, and the vats of the wine-presses are already beginning to receive the juice, and ere long they shall be running full.

For the times of the Gentiles are drawing to a close, and I come. Yea, be thou ready, for I come quickly.

Be Not Afraid

O My child, rest in Me.
Yea, quietly settle down in My care, as a bird settles in a nest.
For I am watching over thee, and in love will I care for thee.

There is no danger with which I am unable to cope.
There is no enemy too formidable for Me to handle.
I am able to carry out all My purposes,
and to keep thee at the same time.

Be not afraid;
neither allow terror to strike at thy heart.
My power is at thy disposal.
My presence standeth round about thee,
and nothing can harm thee so long as ye are in My care,
and that is forever . . .

Seize Each Opportunity

Behold, as the lilies of the field, and as the grass,
so thy life is but for a season.
Yea, though thou flourish in health, yet is thy time short.
Thou hast no sure promise of tomorrow.
Therefore live each day as though it were thy last.
Seize each opportunity knowing it may be the last.

For it is verily true that no situation presents itself twice the
same. The opportunities of today are not those of tomorrow.
Live not as though they might be repeated.
Fail not to enter every open door. Be not held back by a
feeling of unreadiness. I Myself am thy preparation.

For I will give to thee the needed grace and wisdom for each
moment as it cometh, and thou shalt rejoice in the victory.
For I will overcome timidity, and I Myself will displace
inadequacy.
This is *My* work. I will do it Myself through thee if thou
but allow thyself to be a channel for the flow of My Spirit.

90

For I Myself am the life. I Myself am thy wisdom and thy strength,
even as I am thy joy and thy peace.
I am thy victory. My word is power because My word is spirit
and truth.
Do not bear about needless burdens.
They will but press upon thy spirit and interfere with My movings.
Much remains to be accomplished.
Linger not over what appears to be an unfinished case. Pass on.
My Spirit will continue to strive though thou give no further
thought. This way thy mind shall be kept free and thy path open,
and it shall be ever a new way.
Keep ever moving, and from life to life I will accomplish My
purpose.
And know that as I work, all things work together, so that
there is gathering strength and there shall be a glorious
consummation. Praise God!

The Art of Committal

O My child, lay your heart in My hand, and let Me heal it.
Yea, let Me gather up thy tears, for they are precious to Me.
(Psalms 56:8) Ye have not been suffering alone, but I Myself
have been near thee all along the way. My heart has felt all
that ye have felt. Ye do not have a high priest who is not able
to sympathize with your sufferings, but one who experienced
every grief and human emotion common to man. And yet, in the
midst of these experiences of suffering, He did not sin. Therefore,
He is one who is able to succour thee. (Heb. 2:18)

He is one, who having walked the same path Himself, is
able to teach thee how that in the midst of these human experiences
of hurts and frustrations and loneliness and heart-ache, ye may
rise above the natural tendencies to fall into the sins of self-pity,
self-reproach, depression of spirit, resentments and the like.

It is not easy. Not only is it not easy, but in the natural, in
the flesh, it is impossible. But the same grace which I promised to
the apostle Paul to help him bear his affliction, this same grace
I will give to you. (II Cor. 12:9)

Ye may bring the whole of your burden to Me. I will help you as the days go by, and as the trials come and go; and as the learning process continues, I will teach you the spiritual secrets of the art of committal.

For in complete and repeated committal lies the key to victories that can be thus more easily won, less painfully achieved, and more quickly gained, so that the valleys become less deep and less dark, and more quickly passed through.

'Man is born', it is written, 'to trouble, as the sparks fly upward'. (Job 5:7) This is true as surely as rain falls and snow is cold. But it is equally true, and gloriously so, that I have promised, and I will deliver thee out of all thy troubles.

So will ye now take the first step in this experience of committal, and give Me your heart?

Make it as tangible a transaction as possible, and visualize your own hand laying the physical organ of your heart in My hands. Say to Me, "Take this, Loving Master and Wonderful Lord, and do with it as pleases Thee."

'He healeth the broken in heart and bindeth up their wounds.' (Psalms 147:3)

Whatsoever Ye Sow

How can I give you healing for your body whilst there is anxiety in thy mind? So long as there is dis-ease in thy thoughts, there shall be disease in thy body. Ye have need of many things, but one thing in particular ye must develop for thine own preservation, and that is an absolute confidence in My loving care.

'Come unto Me', it is written, 'all ye that labor and are heavy-laden, and I will give you rest.' (Matt. 11:28) Only when your mind is at rest can your body build health. Worry is an actively destructive force. Anxiety produces tension, and tension is the road to pain. Fear is devastating to the physical well-being of the body. Anger throws poison into the system that no anti-biotic ever can counteract.

'Be sure your sin will find you out', the Bible states. One of the most common ways that hidden sin is revealed is through the maladies of the body. More arthritis is brought about by resentments and ill-will than is caused by wrong diet. More asthma is caused by repressed fury than by pollen or cat fur.

There was no illness in the body of Jesus because there was no sin in His soul. There was weariness as a natural result of labor and sacrificial service, but there was no undue fatigue and exhaustion brought on by anxiety.

Ten minutes of unbridled temper can waste enough strength to do a half day of wholesome work. Your physical energy is a gift from God, entrusted to you to be employed for His glory. It is a sin to take His gift and dissipate it through the trap doors of the evil emotions of the disposition.

Look not upon others and condemn them for jeopardizing their health by harmful habits and wasting their energies on vain pursuits while you yourself undermine your health by unworthy emotions and take time which by keeping your mind in an attitude of praise and faith could be constructively employed, but instead you allow this time to be a period of destructive action by entertaining such things as self-pity and remorse and evil-surmisings.

You cannot risk giving your thoughts free-rein. They will never choose the right path until you bridle them and control them by your own disciplined will. You are master of your own house. You do not have to invite into your mind the foul birds of evil thoughts and allow them to nest there and bring forth their young.

Whatsoever ye sow in your secret thought-life, that shall ye reap. Sow love and kindness, and ye shall be rewarded openly. Sow charity and forgiveness, and ye shall reap in kind. Sow generosity and gratitude, and ye shall never feel poor. Sow hope, and ye shall reap fulfillment. Sow praise, and ye shall reap joy and well-being and a strong faith. Sow bountifully, and ye shall reap bountifully. Sow! Ye shall see your seed and be satisfied.

. . .'Scanty sowing, scanty harvest; plentiful sowing, plentiful harvest.' . . . And he who supplies 'seed to the sower, and bread for eating,' will supply you with seed, and cause it to increase, and will multiply 'the fruits of your righteousness'.

(taken from II Cor. 9:6-12 Twentieth Century N. T.)

Chastening

Have I not said that unless ye experience chastening, ye may well doubt thy sonship? Why then, shouldst thou shrink from My rod of correction? Ye are not the teacher, but the pupil; not the parent, but the child; not the vine, but the branch.

Discipline and correction must come if ye would be brought into conformity to My divine will. Shun nothing My hand brings to bear upon thy life. Accept My blessings and My comfort, but do not despise My sterner dealings. All are working toward thy ultimate perfection.

Do ye hope to be made perfect apart from the corrective process? Do ye expect to bear large fruit without the pruning process? Nay, My children, either bend in submission to My hand, or ye shall break in rebellion.

Godly sorrow yieldeth the good fruit of repentance, but if ye be brittle and unyielding, ye shall know a grief of spirit for which there is no remedy. Keep a flexible spirit, so that I may mold thee and shape thee freely — so that I can teach thee readily, nor be detained by thy resistance.

I need disciplined Christians. To entertain self-will is to court disqualification. Ye cannot do My work to My satisfaction except ye do it in accordance with My specifications. There are not many blueprints for one building; there is only one. Even so, to change the figure, there are not many different husbandmen. *I* am the husbandman. If ye refuse My loving care of thee, ye shall be cut down by others who have no concern for thy soul. Even as I said of the salt: if it lose its savor, it is good for naught but shall be trodden under foot of man. If the branch bear no fruit, men shall gather it and burn it.

Do not relax in a false peace. Do not negate My love by refusing My discipline. My love is not indulgence. I have much to accomplish in fulfilling My will. I cannot pamper your will when it is running counter to Mine.

Be no longer spoiled children, allowing the emotions of the old nature to invade your spiritual fellowships. For while there are jealousies and competition and suspicions, ye are yet allowing the carnal nature to reign — even to infiltrate thy spiritual gifts.

The Last Great Outpouring

Behold, ye stand on the threshold of a new day. For I have truly great things in store for thee. Yea, thou hast not power to conceive that which I am about to do. For I shall bring to pass a new thing. Thou shalt rejoice exceedingly. Ye have heard of the showers, but I say unto thee that I shall send a mighty downpour. Many have cried unto Me out of hungry hearts and have received of My fulness and seen My glory; but I say unto thee, that in the day of the great deluge that is about to come, many shall come to know the reality of My power who have up until now not even dreamed of such a thing.

Many who are scoffers, and many who are honest doubters shall find themselves swept away on the swelling tide of the outpouring of the Holy Spirit. For this is the time of the last great outpouring. This is the day of the preparation for the coming of the Lord. Many shall rejoice together in the Spirit's work who now are even at sword's point over doctrinal disputations and barriers of tradition.

But let thine heart be encouraged; for a new day is dawning: a day of repentance and a day of gathering for My people, saith the Lord. For they shall not continue barricaded and isolated behind walls of prejudice. I am the LORD, and I will be worshipped in spirit and in truth, and not in the bigotry of sectarianism and narrowness of denominationalism. The world is waiting for a robust Church to minister to its needs; and how can an ailing, dismembered Body bring healing to a sick and dying world?

Surely I will pour out My Spirit, and by prophecies, by signs and wonders, by many different types of miracles, and by healings, I will reaffirm the veracity of My Word and bring the message of the Gospel of Redemption to many who would otherwise never give heed. I am the Alpha and the Omega. Stand firm in Me. Never waver.

Be faithful regardless of apparent failures and discouragements; for My word shall surely be fulfilled, and thine eyes shall see Revival in proportion like as has never been witnessed before in the history of the human race.

Keep your eye on the end of the course. Victory is secured already. Do not let the hurdles cause thee consternation. Stay in the running. Verily, I am at thy side. According to each day shall thy strength be; and the race is not to the swift, but the obedient shall receive the prize.

Sing, My Children

O My people, My chosen ones, I love thee with an ever-lasting love, and with the cords of My faithfulness have I bound thee unto Myself. I am not a man that I should lie, (Num. 23:19), but all I have promised to thee, that I will surely do, to the end that the Father may be glorified in thee, and that ye may bear much fruit.

I have promised thee My grace, in order that ye may extend to others that love such as Mine, that flows forth in the face of hostility. When ye were at enmity with God, Christ died for thee. Calvary love was given not for friends, but for enemies. I would teach you how to love with Calvary love.

Remember that I am in the midst when ye praise me. Never let any kind of anxiety crowd out thy praises. Do not be concerned for My reputation. I have withstood many a storm, and I will survive this one. Man's strivings are as the waters around Gibraltar. They have beat upon the rock, but they have not changed it. I am not disturbed, and I forbid thee to be anxious.

For anxiety gendereth to tension, and tension erodes joy; and when joy is gone, victory is lost, faith is weakened, and spontaneity is destroyed. The spirit falls ill. The salt has lost its flavor. Its savor is a saver. What can I use to preserve My work in your midst if ye lose your JOY?

Rejoice *always*, said the apostle Paul — and again I say *rejoice*. Let your stability be observable to all men, for truly, the coming of the Lord is near. Gird up your loins, and be strong; for it is the Lord who upholdeth thee, and He it is who giveth thee the victory.

Sing, My children, and let the shout of praise be heard; for the Lord is mighty, and His Name is glorious.

LEARN TO REIGN

"Till we all come in the unity of the faith, and of the knowledge of the Son of God unto a perfect man, unto the measure of the stature of the fulness of Christ."

Ephesians 4:13

Contents

"Tender Dove" 103

Quiet Pool 104

Call of the Turtledove 106

Love Never Faileth 107

Hold Fast 108

Thou Hast Run Into My Arms 109

I Anticipate Thy Dependence Upon Me 110

Lie Not Dormant 112

As Rains of Refreshing 113

Head Into the Wind 114

The Mind of God 116

I Have Planned Ahead for Thee 117

Dynamos of Praise 118

I Shall Rejoice In My People 119

Grow Up In Me 120

Walk Ye In It 121

Jewels 122

I Joy Over Thee 123

Learn to Reign 124

Open Thine Heart to Me 127

Fortitude 128

On Doing The Father's Work 128

"Tender Dove"

Holy Spirit from above,
Tender, undefiled Dove,
In my spirit have Thy way,
O'er my actions hold full sway.

Blest Companion from on high,
In Thy comfort ever nigh;
Bind my heart to Christ in love,
O Thou precious, Heavenly Dove.

This cold heart and these dull eyes,
So unfit for Paradise,
Fire with Thy sacred flame,
Show the power of Jesus' Name.

Weak I in myself may be,
But my strength shall be in Thee.
Sweet provision of God's grace;
In Thy gift His love I trace.

I could not Thy coming earn,
Could no more Thy wooing spurn.
Take control and bless and use
As the Infinite shall choose.

—FJR

103

Quiet Pool

Lo, I say unto thee, Wait upon ME.
Let thy life be as a deep, quiet pool.
Yea, let thine heart rest in Mine hand as a bird in a nest.
Let thine eyes be still. Let thine hands be free.
    For then shall I fill all thy vision,
    and then shall I take thine hands into Mine
    and My power shall flow forth unto thee.

Only make unto thyself a place apart;
yea, a place removed from the press and turmoil,
and there will I meet thee. Yea I wait thy coming.
    For I long to pour out my blessings upon thee,
        and I long to give thee of my fulness.
        Only be thou still before Me.
    Let not the toils and cares of the day
    rob thee of this sweet fellowship with Me.

For I know what things ye have need of, and I am
concerned about thine every duty and responsibility.
    But thou wilt find thy cares have vanished
    and thy load lightened as by an unseen hand.
    For I will that ye bring Me thy love,
    and even as thou art bringing to Me thy love,
    I shall in turn bring to thee My power,
    so that I work for thee in a two-fold measure.

For I give unto thee the power to discharge thy duties with greater efficiency, and I also am actively engaged in working for thee in ways thou canst not see, to make thy path clear, and to bring about things which thou thyself couldest never accomplish, and which would otherwise absorb thine energies and wear out thy patience.

So I say unto thee again . . . Rest in Me. Wait upon Me. Come apart with me. Seek My face. Seek my fellowship.

———

O Lord, what shame that Thou shouldest need to beg us thus! Sooner might others seek to find us available and be unable because of our occupation with Thee, rather than this — that we are so slow to come, so dull to hear, so cold of heart, so indolent of soul.

O God, spare us Thy wrath!
Let not Thine anger be kindled against us.
Let us ask but one thing more, and turn not away.

Grant this one prayer more, O Lord, even that Thou wouldest give to us all that is lacking in us; that Thou wilt make our wills to will; that Thou wilt intensify our hunger and fire our devotion, and take the indifference from our spirits, and have Thy wonderful way and perfect will, O God, we pray.

Amen.

Call of the Turtledove

O My children, there is the sound of the turtledove going throughout the land. It is the voice of the Bridegroom calling forth His Bride. It is the wooing of the Spirit bringing forth a people for His Name. Yea, it is the Lord of Glory, Jesus Christ Himself, drawing together them that are His. It is the call of love, and they who truly love Him shall respond.

Like attracts like; and love has ever been the test of true discipleship. Those whose hearts are fixed on things above shall not be holden by worldly entanglements (even though these be in the organized church). They who are listening to the voice of their Beloved shall not be deafened by the cries of men. In a world that is filled with noises, each demanding attention, they shall hear.

Yea, they shall even hear the tender cooing of the turtledove! Another may stand beside them and hear only the voice of the preacher. Another may be giving attention to the opinions and arguments of men. In the words of the beloved hymn-writer: "The love of Jesus, what it is, None but His loved ones know."

Ye need not fear that ye will miss it. Be it ever so soft, ye shall hear. Lo, thy heart shall hear, and thy heart shall leap with joy. Ye shall be even as Elizabeth when greeted by Mary. The response was immediate — an inner, involuntary response to the nearness of the Christ, even while He was yet unborn and unseen by the world.

I tell you, there shall be a revelation of My nearness given to My dear ones before My second coming.

Anticipate Me. Watch for Me. Thy heart shall listen, and thy heart shall hear. I am not far off. I am looking through the lattice.* Ye shall see Me — ye shall know — ye shall rejoice.
*Song of Solomon 2:9

106

Love Never Faileth

Behold, I am the Lord, *Thy* God; is *anything* too hard for Me? I am the LIGHT of the world, and the greatest darkness shall never be able to quench that light. I shall be to thee a cloud to preserve by day and a pillar of fire to protect by night. Both in the sunshine and in the darkness, I shall be near thee. Thou shalt delight in Me in thy joys; and in the place of difficulty My love for thee shall be as inescapably real as a blazing pillar of fire. Yea, all I was to Israel, and more, I shall be to thee. For have I not promised to give thee the desires of thine heart, and the heathen for thine inheritance?

Let *no fear* hinder. For he that wavereth receiveth not. But keep thine heart single and every alien thought thou shalt rebuke in My Name, for it is of the enemy. For he knoweth full well that he has no defense against pure faith. Only if he can succeed to plant some seed of doubt can he hold back the blessing of heaven among the people of God and nullify the witness to the lost. So hold fast thy profession of FAITH, for there is a great recompense of reward. (Or we may say, the inheritance of faith is a most rewarding recompense.)

So praise Me continually, for *Praise* worketh *Faith,* and *God inhabiteth the Praise of His People.* If ever I seem to be far from thee, *PRAISE!* If ever darkness seemeth to press about thee, this know, — thou hast neglected to PRAISE ME. Love ME; pour out thy adoration and worship. Be sure of this: *LOVE NEVER FAILETH.* Loving Me never fails to bring Me to thy side. He seeth Me most clearly who lovest Me most dearly.

Hold Fast

Hold fast that which thou hast, and let no man take thy crown.
Let no man hinder thee in pursuit of the reward.
Let nothing stand in the way of thy complete victory.
Let no weariness or discouraging thought cause thee to un-
loose the rope of faith,
but bind it the tighter and anchor fast to My Word.

For My Word can never fail,
yea, and all My good promises I will surely fulfill.
Have not I said, 'He that seeketh shall find'? And have not
I promised to be the rewarder of them that diligently seek Me?
Not of the dilatory seeker, but of the diligent seeker.
Not of him whose seeking is in reality only wishing, but of
him who has grown so intent in his quest that he has become
wholly absorbed to the extent that he is unmindful in his toiling
of the sweat upon his brow.
To the extent that he has ceased reckoning the cost,
indeed, verily, has quit offering bribes,
as though the fulness of God might be purchased,
and has set out on foot,
deserting all else to follow the call of the Spirit until . . .

Until hunger is swallowed up in fulness.
Until heart-cry is answered by the voice of God through His
mighty Holy Spirit.
Until all the emptiness and loneliness of the subterranian re-
cesses of his soul
are flooded by the sublime, glorious reality of Emmanuel.
Emmanuel! God with us—God in us—God in me!—God in you!
Praise His holy, wonderful Name! For this He made us.
For this He destined us! For this He predestinated us!
For this He died and rose.
For this He sent that first mighty outpouring at Pentecost.
Praise God! Praise God!

Never stifle the cry in your heart. God put it there.
God puts no special premium on our being perennial spiritual
      Pollyannas.
His joy springs forth most abundantly
      in souls that have been soaked in tears.
Not the tears of self-pity. Never.
But the tears of devotion and longing after Him.
Weep. But when you weep, weep in His arms.
Doubt if you must, but tell each doubt to Him candidly.
You will be surprised how quickly they will melt away.
      His love and His smile will dispel every doubt
      as silently and surely as sunshine removes frost.
You cannot look in His face and doubt at the same time!

Thou Hast Run Into My Arms

O My child, thou hast thought in thine heart that thou wouldst run from Me. But lo, I am everywhere before thee, and thou hast only run into My arms. For I care for thee — yea, I think upon thee constantly, and I seek to do thee good.

Thou fearest My rod of correction, but as it is written, it is the love of God that causes men to repent. Take My love, and in the taking, thy heart shall be so warmed and made tender, and at the same time encouraged and made strong, that ye will not need the rod, nor anticipate My displeasure.

For if it be so that human love covereth a multitude of sins (I Pe. 4:8) how much more is it true of the divine love of God the Father! Knowing My deep love for thee, thine own heart shall no longer condemn thee. My mercies are everlasting, and My kindness abundant.

My grace extendeth unto the least of My children, and My tenderness shall make thee strong. I go before thee daily to prepare thy way, and thou shalt be accompanied by My goodness and My mercy.

I Anticipate Thy Dependence Upon Me

O My son, give Me thy heart, for out of it are the issues of life. For I say unto thee, My hand is upon thee, and I will keep thee in all places whithersoever thou goest. Yea, I am thy God, and I am thy father, and I shall care for thee and provide for thee according to all that thou needest. Yea, and I shall be at thy side, ready to help thee whenever thou shalt call upon Me. I am not unmindful of any of thy needs, and My concern is for thee.

Thou dost not need to carry thine own load, for I will be happy to help thee carry it and to also bear thee up as well. Thou dost not walk alone nor meet any situation alone, for I am with thee, and I will give thee wisdom and I will give thee strength, and My blessing shall be upon thee. Only keep thine heart set upon Me and thine affections on things above; for I cannot bless thee unless ye ask Me and I cannot answer if ye do not call, and I cannot minister to thee except thou come to Me.

Do not wait to feel more worthy, for no man is worthy of My blessings. My grace bypasses all thy shortcomings, and I give to My children because they ask of Me and because I love them, and I do not love one more than another. I give most liberally to those who ask the most of Me. For I love to have thee depend upon Me. This is why the Spirit within thee crieth 'Abba — Father.' As thy *father* I anticipate thy dependence upon Me. Thou mayest by maturity outgrow thy dependence upon human parentage, but as My child, ye shall never "outgrow" thy spiritual sonship, nor shall I ever cast thee upon thine own resources, even when thou shalt thyself come into this position of father in human relationship. Thou shalt then appreciate even more fully My feelings toward thee. For thou shalt know by thine own human experience the love of a father, and the desire to care for and provide, and ye shall know more fully how much I love thee, and how ready I am to help thee, and how available I am to counsel with thee and give thee My support.

Heaven's resources are at thy command, and thou needest never to want, so long as I am thy Shepherd. Think not in thine heart that since I know all about thee, thou needest not tell Me. It is true that I know, but ye need to tell Me so that in the telling ye may experience the release of an open heart, and the fellowship of a Friend.

For as ye open your heart to Me, I will come to thee. As ye speak to Me, I will speak to you. As ye reveal thyself to Me, I will reveal Myself to you. This is a law of life. There must be action to bring reaction. There must be a question to bring an answer. There must be an expression of love and confidence on the part of one person to arouse a corresponding response in another person.

Never presume upon My presence. Never assume that knowing thy need, I will automatically supply. *Ask,* and it shall be given. *Call* upon Me, and I will answer thee. *Tell Me* that you love Me, and I will make thy heart to know in a very real way My love for thee and My nearness, and thou shalt never feel alone.

Welcome Me into your heart, and the more ye sense My presence within thee, the more ye shall feel at home no matter where ye may be. Forget anything else, but never forget this.

Lie Not Dormant

My child, I have need of thee. Without thy active help, I am hampered in My work, even as a human body is handicapped by the ineffective operation of any particular member, however small or insignificant. Thou canst not lie idle without hindering the ministry of the Church as a corporate body. Yea, thou canst not move independently of My Spirit without causing damage to the harmonious working of the whole; for by My Spirit is oneness of thought and of action produced. Lie not dormant. Be not slothful, neither allow thyself to sleep.

For we know that the whole world lieth in a sleep of death in the lap of the wicked one, as a child napping unsuspecting in a death-trap. But be thou watchful and diligent and alert, for the time is at hand. Let him that is married be as though he were single, and let him that is entangled in extraneous activities disengage himself; and keep thyself free for the guidance and use of the Spirit of God, even as He directeth thee moment by moment.

My hand shall be upon thee, and My energy shall be at thy disposal, and thou shalt be partaker of My joy. Yea, My peace shall fortify thy thought life, and I shall give health and strength to thy bones. My love shall be thy constant portion. For I ask thee not to labour in drudgery, but the work of God is a labour of love, for God is love; and as ye live by the motivation of My Spirit, ye shall be partaker continually of My life, and thou shalt experience the comforting warmth of My love and My divine presence. For I am with thee and in thee both to will and to do of My good pleasure. This also thou mayest share, and My pleasure is perpetual, whereas the pleasures of the world and all the joys of the natural man are but for a moment.

So I say to thee again, as I have said to thee before: This is the Way, WALK ye in it. Turn not to the left hand nor to the right, and the Lord Thy God shall be to thee even Elohim — the "God Who Revealeth Himself," and I shall reveal Myself to thee in a richer and fuller measure than thou hast known Me hitherto. And thou shalt know that there is not, and never can be, any exhausting of My resources. Nay, Thou canst with naked eye never begin to discover the vastness of the physical universe. For all My creative work in nature is not a beginning of all that I am in Myself. How canst thou comprehend the Love of God? For Paul prayed even to this end, that ye might know the scope of the Love of God. What an area of Infinitude awaits thee!

So move out, and move on, and thou shalt find greater heights ever before thee. Unknown riches await thy discovery and unimagined joys thine experience. As Paul, learn to keep the physical under due and proper control in order that the Spirit may not in any way be restricted; for the Spirit warreth against the flesh, and the flesh is ever at enmity with the Spirit. Be not overcome of evil, but squeeze out the unprofitable things by an abundance of good.

Lo, I am with thee, and I will help thee. Be not discouraged, neither weary of heart, for he reapeth who faints not.

As Rains of Refreshing

As rains of refreshing, O Lord,

So pour out Thy Spirit upon our waiting hearts.

As showers upon new-mown hay,

O send Thy Spirit upon our thirsty souls.

For upon Thee, O God, do we wait.

Satisfy our hungering souls with Thine abundance.

Yea, fill Thou our longing hearts with Thy fulness.

For in Thy presence is fulness of Joy;

At Thy right hand are eternal pleasures.

Head Into The Wind

O My beloved, be not anxious concerning tomorrow. Thou shalt encounter nothing of which I am not already cognizant. My mercy is concealed within every storm cloud. My grace flows beneath every cross-current. My wisdom has conceived a solution to every perplexity.

I have deliberately set obstacles in thy path to test thy prowess. I shall not always cause favorable winds to blow upon thy barque, for then ye would be at ease and would soon grow soft and dull. It is when the wind is high and the waves are threatening that ye become alert and keen, and thus I can strengthen your spiritual fiber.

The storm is not a thing to fear but rather to welcome. Ye shall learn to head into the wind with sheer delight as soon as ye have made the discovery that in the time of stress and strain, ye have the clearest revelations of Myself.

Was it not true of the disciples? Looking out across the raging waters, what did they see? Was it not Jesus? Jesus — *coming unto them!* To have had this happen only once, would have been worth weathering many storms.

In the midst of the multi-heated fiery furnace, what saw the three Hebrew lads? Was it not the living form of Jesus Christ Himself having come to join company with them? Yea, He shone so bright to them that His brilliance obliterated the sight of the flames!

Nay, ye need have no fear. Ye need not fear the fickleness of providence — for behind all that looks to thee like utter chaos, I have a plan which is working for good in thy behalf.

Ye need never fear as to whether I will be faithful to thee, for if I have never failed anyone else, why would I fail thee? Ye have an innumerable company of spectators cheering thee from the ramparts of heaven, reminding you of what I did for them, and encouraging you that the struggle is not interminable, but surprisingly soon it shall end in victory for you also — if ye endure faithful.

Do ye fear the weakness within thine own self? Lo, I have put it there to drive thee to Myself. I may never answer thy prayers to be made strong, but I *will* give you the same promise I gave Paul, that in your weakness I will be your strength. For it is still true that My grace operates most effectively when ye have a conscious sense of need — yea, even a desperate awareness of your own complete helplessness.

Miracles burst forth out of the moist, cold soil of human tragedy. Moist with tears, and cold with hopelessness. I never get a chance to do miracles for you when you are occupied with self-realization, — while ye are entertaining ideas about what wonderful thing I am going to make out of *you*. I do not use *you* for material for miracles; I make miracles out of My own Being. I allow you to watch Me after ye thoroughly understand that it is *I* who am supernatural, not you.

You do not have to be other than what I created you: human. You are only obligated to do that for which I created you: glorify Me. Stand back! Let God be God. Let man be man. Once ye accept your limitations and settle the fact once and for all that I will never ask you to perform Herculean feats, ye can begin to learn what I really have in mind for you.

I am not discouraged with you, but ye will become discouraged with yourself if ye are not able to comprehend the truth of what I taught through Paul, that it is the foolish whom I use to confound the wise, and the things which are nothing, to shatter man's pride in the things which he has made himself.

I *am* the Ruler, and I *will* reign. Ye can resist Me, but it shall inevitably be to thine own destruction. Love Me and trust Me, and stay in a place of humility. As it is written, "Humble thyself under the mighty hand of God, and He will raise thee up." Mind you, *He* will do it. Ye need not raise yourself.

You need only stay humble.

The Mind of God

O My child, give Me your mind. I shall keep it in perfect tranquility. Give Me your thoughts. I will keep them in peace. If ye allow other people to do thy thinking for thee, thou shalt be distressed. If ye try to do it for thyself, ye may be in error through limited knowledge or mis-information. But let the mind of Christ be in you. Let My thinking displace and supersede thy mind and thy reasonings, and thou shalt be kept in peace and order and shalt know exactly and precisely what is right, what is true, and what is the proper course of action.

As ye draw upon My Spirit for physical strength, so draw upon My Mind for wisdom and understanding and peace of mind. Make this a habit in thy life and thou shalt be astounded at the results, the accomplishments, it will bring. Rather than being motivated by impulse, ye shall be directed by Divine Intelligence.

Have I not promised that if any lack wisdom, they may ask of God who giveth liberally and without discrimination? I have not left you to flounder like a rudderless ship. I will freely share with you all ye need of My thinking powers, even as I share of My grace for the needs of the soul.

This is a reservoir very nearly untapped. This is why I commended Solomon, because he asked the highest gift. In adding the other benefits, I gave him only those things which shall surely always follow after this first. For the life truly directed by My Mind shall enjoy in abundance many other blessings.

Ye shall know who hath need of healing, and what the physical need, yes, even what is the true cause of illness, that healing may be complete in the whole man. Ye shall know who is speaking error, and ye shall not only discern the craftiness of the enemy, but know how to rebuke him in My Name.

Ye shall be unafraid before the face of every man, for wisdom is power. Ye shall be unashamed to speak, for ye shall know that the words ye speak are not your own, but His Who has sent thee and made thee His messenger. Yes, you shall be able to testify as did Jesus: the words that I speak, I speak not of myself, but they are the words given me by the Father. Know that I will do it. Trust Me to do it. Ye shall rejoice exceedingly beyond any joy ye have yet experienced.

Amazing things await thee. Ye have had but a tiniest fortaste. Launch out! The mind of God is fathomless. Who can ponder the smallest fraction of the intelligence of the Creator? It is all at thy disposal — a great repository upon which ye may freely draw. Draw, then, for truly 'the well is deep.'

I Have Planned Ahead for Thee

Behold, am I a God that is afar off, and not a God that is near? For in the midst of difficulties, I will be thy support. In the darkness, I am thy light; yea, there is no darkness that the world can produce that can hide My face from the eye of faith. My beauty and My radiance are all the lovelier by the contrast.

In grief, My comfort is the more poignant. In failure, My encouragement the most welcome. In loneliness, the touch of My presence, more tender. Yea, thou art hid in Me; and I will multiply both the wisdom and the strength in due proportion to meet the demands of every occasion.

I am the Lord Thy God. I know no limitations. I know no lack. I need not reserve My stores, for I always have a fresh supply. Thou canst by no means ever exhaust My resources. Let thy heart run wild. Let thine imagination go vagabond. No extravagance of human thought can ever plumb the depths of My planning and provision for My children.

Rejoice, therefore, and face each day with joy; for I have planned ahead for thee, and made all necessary arrangements and reservations. I am thy guide and benefactor. Put your hand in Mine.

Dynamos of Praise

O My child, lean upon Me; for I am thy helper; I am thy shield and thy buckler. Yea, I am thy strong tower and support. No evil shall befall thee, for thou art surrounded and protected by My presence, and no evil can touch Me. Yea, let thine heart rejoice in Me, and occupy thine heart with praise. There is no need that I will not fulfill as ye praise and worship — both your needs and the needs of others.

Man has contemplated the power of faith and of *prayer*, but only rarely have I revealed to men this far greater power of *praise*. For by prayer and faith doors are opened, but by praise and worship, great dynamos of power are set in motion, as when a switch is thrown and an electric power plant such as Niagra is thrown into operation. Praying for specifics is like requesting light for individual houses in various scattered places, while worshipping and praise flood the whole area with available current.

I do not discount prayer (petitions). I only show you a more marvelous way — a faster means of bringing more help to more people with less elapse of time. So many need Me. So little time is available. Turn loose thy praises, and in proportion to thy liberality, ye shall see My generosity expressed, and in infinite magnitude.

Labor not to analyze each need. Leave the diagnosis and the mechanics of it in My hands. Complexities are as nothing to Me. They exist only in thy mind, sown by the enemy, to dull thy faith. Ignore all this. Weigh nothing except the love of My heart. Ask nothing except ye inquire of thine own heart how much love for Me is there. Hold Me closely, nor let Me go. I will surely bless you, and I will make you a blessing.

I will make *you* a blessing. Think not to *take* a blessing to someone, or hope that I will *send* a blessing. Lo, I will make thee, as My ambassador, to be thyself a sweet savour of life and grace. Through thy saltiness shall others be made thirsty. Through thy joy shall others be made to long after reality.

Yea, through thy peace and confidence shall others seek for Me, and they shall themselves find Me even as ye have found Me. I will reveal Myself to them as I have revealed Myself to you. Perhaps in a different way, because each has different needs, but I *will* open to all who knock. I *will* reward those who seek. *I* will reward. Ye need only preserve thy soul's integrity. This is enough to fully occupy thine energies and attention. Leave the miracles to Me. You *be* and I will *do*.

I Shall Rejoice In My People

By My Spirit, saith the Lord, shall I get Me the victory.

By My Spirit shall I open the eyes of the blind;

>for surely I will move, and no hand shall stay Me.

I will break through the locked gates as a flow of flaming lava.

I will not withhold My power and My glory from any seeking heart.

They who desire Me, I will surely reward: I will not fail.

I will fill every longing heart and satisfy every craving soul.

>My grace will I pour out as a tumbling waterfall.

>I shall be glorified, and I shall be magnified,

>>and I shall rejoice in My people, in that day

>when they yield themselves fully and freely to Me:

>>yea, when they give themselves utterly to Me

>>>and cut loose from all beside.

Then shall I cast My love about them as a cloak,

>and I shall whisper My words in their ears.

Grow Up In Me

O My people, I have purposes for thee that embrace eternity. Before the creation of the worlds, I planned for thy redemption, for it is written of the Lord Jesus Christ that He was the Lamb foreordained before the foundation of the world. I Pet. 1:20 Yea, and I have manifested Him to you, so that ye have believed in Him and have been born again, not of corruptible seed but of incorruptible, even that which liveth and abideth forever.

So then, now that ye are in Christ, ye have My life abiding in you, and ye have become a new creation. Grow up in Me now, so that ye may develop in the process of time into the full stature of men and women — even unto the measure of the fulness of Christ.   (Eph. 4:13)

For I have not purposed simply to bring you into My family and have you remain as babes or children. I am concerned with your maturity: your growth in wisdom and knowledge of things pertaining to Myself; with the perfection of your ministry; and with the producing of the fruits of the Spirit in your life.

And so to this end, I have provided for you the *ministries* and *gifts* of My Holy Spirit. As ye receive these by faith, and as ye walk in these by faith, so that I am allowed to manifest Myself through you in this way, ye will find that ye will grow in Me, yea, grow in grace and in your knowledge of Me, and ye will find the *fruits* of the Spirit will begin to appear in thy life quite naturally, even as apples appear on the apple tree, though the tree takes no thought and experiences no effort or anxiety.

Commit to Me thy sanctification. Bring thy thoughts into captivity and let thy mind be under the control of the Mind of Christ. Do not curb the impulses of the Spirit within you, neither refuse to allow Me the freedom to manifest Myself through you by means of the gifts. Ye may resist Me, because ye feel unworthy or 'unready' to be used. This is a delusion of the mind. I do not use you when you 'feel prepared' but when I need you and you are yielded. Even as I use you, ye will discover that in the process of being used, I shall do a work in you yourself to the edification of your own heart and life.

So then, ye block the way to your own spiritual development if ye hold Me back when I would minister through you.

(Ephesians 4:12 & 16)

Indeed, if the time should ever come that ye 'feel ready', I would then be completely blocked by your pride, and would be forced to use someone else.

Walk Ye In It

Behold, I say unto thee,
This is the way. Walk ye in it.

Lo, I am the way.
Walk in Me.
I am the truth. *Believe Me* (trust in Me).
I am the Life. *Live in Me*, and share My life with others.

For thou knowest not what I do now,
but thou shalt know hereafter.
(Now we see in a glass darkly, but then, face to face. Now our grasp of the ways of God is incomplete, but as we move on, we come to understand what He has been endeavoring to do in our lives.)

Rejoice.
Rejoice not so much in victories as in the fact that I am leading.
Praise Me.
Not so much for My blessings as for My love which prompts them.
Serve Me with gladness,
not for the ultimate nor present reward,
but for the thrill of knowing that we labor together;
that I stand beside thee in every enterprise however trivial.

Jewels

O My Bride, My Beloved:

I have betrothed thee unto Myself. Yea, I have given thee a special token of our relationship and our future union, for I have sealed thee with My precious Holy Spirit; and ye shall be Mine, saith the Lord, in that day when I make up My jewels, and ye shall be as a diadem upon My brow, yea, My crowning glory.

For I shall reign over kings and nations and peoples, yea, I shall be ruler over all the earth; but ye shall have a special place of honor, for thou art My prize possession. As it is written, having shared My agony, ye shall that day share My glory; having born for Me the cross, ye shall then share with Me the throne. (Know ye not ye shall even judge angels?)

Rejoice now, that ye have been chosen out and counted worthy to suffer for My sake. We share one common destiny, and we walk one single path. At this present time, it may hold sorrow and isolation; but cheer thine heart with the raptures that lie ahead. Some live now in the revelries and riches of this present world who shall that day be mourners and paupers. Will ye exchange places? Would ye desert Me now and be rejected then? Would ye ignore Me now, and be in that day rejected by Me?

Nay, ye would not! Rather, ye will do as Paul: ye will glory in the midst of suffering and affliction, because ye know these things shall in that day be counter-balanced by an exceedingly greater portion of joy. (weight of glory)

I Joy Over Thee

My son, My little one, My under-shepherd, My dear friend: — you are many things to Me, even as I am many things to you. My love for you is deep and tender. I know thy desire to please Me, and I am happy that it is so. How can I tell thee that though I desire holiness, and while I desire fruit in thy life, still My love for thee is in nowise contingent upon any attainment? My glory is involved in the way ye live. Eternal destinies are involved in the matters of thy holiness and thy faithfulness and thine obedience to My direction and will; but My love for thee is independent of these factors.

I love thee because you are My child. I love thee because I am your Father. I love you with Calvary love. At great price have I redeemed thee: this I did because I loved thee. When I planned this, I foresaw thee lost in sin, and I loved thee and chose thee and set My heart upon thee.

Rather than struggling to comprehend the working of My sovereignty, accept this, and rejoice in it, and draw near to Me without spoiling the preciousness of our fellowship with any shadows of self-condemnation.

You are Mine, and I joy over thee. Discipline I reserve for the rebellious. The first step of repentance brings My mercy.

> "Mercy there is great, and grace is free —
> Pardon there is multiplied to thee,
> There the burdened heart finds liberty at Calvary."

Let the peace of God rule in your heart and mind, and be filled with thanksgiving.

Learn to Reign

Call My people to repentance. Yea, call them to their knees for prayer and fasting, for confession and vigilance. For this is a strategic hour. The enemy is rejoicing already over his anticipated victories. Ye can disappoint him and thwart his evil designs if ye lay hold upon the throne of God in steadfast, believing prayer.

Yea, I say unto thee, ye must do even as the devil has done and anticipate your victories in advance. Ye can do MORE than the enemy at this point. For ye can claim the victories in the Name of Jesus, and all that ye claim in that all-powerful Name is sealed in Heaven before it comes to pass on earth, and the enemy is defeated, yea, even prior to the actual battle.

Lay hold upon this, My people. This is not only a glorious truth in which to rejoice, but it is *absolutely vital to thy victory.* How go the troops to battle in carnal warfare? Not without due preparation, ample ammunition, and intensive training. I do not expect you to meet your adversary unequipped, unarmed, undisciplined.

Do not count upon Me to deliver by some kind of magic. I give you orders and ye must obey, otherwise ye shall suffer intolerable defeat. Ye do not face light skirmishes in which you can look for easy victories. I remind you that you are not contending with flesh and blood and matching wits with men, but ye are being ambushed and facing open attack from the very enemy of your souls, Satan himself.

He is not out to torment. He is out to destroy. Not to hurt you, but to crush you. Your strength is no match against him. Ye *must* learn how to lay claim to the *throne* of God. *I* have met him and won already as I hung on the cross. *Now YOU* must find the way of victory yourselves — each one individually — so that My victory already won can become a present victory in operation for you.

Do not cry to Me in the hour of crisis and distress as though I would extend some miracle in answer to prayer. Of course, I *do* answer prayer, and I can perform miracles, and bring deliverance, but if I do this, I have only rescued one of my own out of trouble while you yourself have won no victory at all! I want to teach you how to actually circumvent the enemy — to drive him out of the arena. How to subdue kingdoms and how to truly reign in the kingdom of heaven. I want you to experience Jericho's — not Ai's. Ye *must* be OVERCOMERS if My work is to be accomplished.

Ye are not qualified to be used for My purposes as long as ye are being harassed by the enemy and I keep needing to rescue you from a constant parade of distressing predicaments. Ye are MORE THAN CONQUERORS, Paul said, and it was by My Spirit that Paul was taught to speak thus.

Rise up, then, and lay claim to the power that is yours, because I am in you, and ye are in Me, and as I was in the world, even so are ye. I was victorious, and you too may be victorious. I withstood every encounter with the devil, and you too can stand against him. I healed the sick and wrested tortured bodies out of the grip of evil forces, and you too can do the same.

LEARN TO REIGN, for lo, I have made you to become kings and priests. I have purposed that ye should come into that place where ye share My authority and thus I will be able to manifest forth My glory through you. This is My greatest joy — to lift man out of enemy territory, and seat him in the heavenlies with Me. And where am I? Even at the right hand of the Father who sitteth upon the throne, and He has invested in Me all power in heaven and earth and under the earth; and Ye are seated with Me, far above all principalities and powers. Through Me ye have inherited all. And ye can lay claim to that inheritance *now* because I have already died. Because I have already died, ye can enter in *now*. You do not gain an inheritance when *you* die, but when the testator dies. *Take it*, My people. It is yours *now*. It is yours because of Calvary. When ye think of Calvary ye think of My love; and this indeed is the tie-in between Calvary and this sharing of My throne life. I want you with Me. I want you seated beside Me because I want you near Me. Because I love you.

Where do you expect to see a queen? Beside the king. I have not spoken of you as such, but ye are My Bride. A queen is subordinate to a king, and he reigns while she stands by. No, ours is a closer relationship, for I have vested you with authority also. Ye reign with Me if it be so that ye recognize your privilege to do so, and if ye move out in the power of the Spirit into that realm where I would have you to live and move and, yes, to have your very being. For I would have a people who live in Me continually, and not that ye be moving in and out of this place. I would have you live continually in the center of the kingdom of God, just as I have placed the Kingdom within the very center of your being. You bring this kingdom into operation in your own life by an act of faith; yea, verily, by a constant attitude of faith. For saith the Lord: I will have Me a people in these last days through whom I can manifest My glory. There are works which I must yet do through My body, the Church, which I could not possibly have accomplished through My own physical body in My earthly ministry. I am even now bringing this body together, uniting the individual members, breathing My breath into it, empowering with gifts and ministries, in order that through it I may do My work. So that when the time comes that I take the church out of the world, I may be able to say again "It is finished."

Know this also, that there are sufferings yet to be accomplished in the body of the Church that I was not able to suffer on the cross. Did not Paul write "that ye fill up what is lacking of the sufferings of Christ"?* Lo, I write unto you now that ye be patient, and that ye hold steady through the days that lie ahead, and know that the trials and suffering are working toward a consuming glory.

PRAISE ME, O MY PEOPLE, PRAISE ME. Praise Me out of a heart full of love. Praise Me for every blessing and every victory. Yea, and Praise Me when the most difficult thing to do is to Praise. This is the victory that overcometh the world, even your faith, and praise is the voice of faith. It is faith rejoicing for victories claimed in advance. The song of praise is made

*Col. 1:24

of the very fabric of things hoped for. It becomes an evidence of unseen things. It is the raw material in My hands from which I fashion your victories.

Give it to me. Give Me much, give to Me often. I dwell in the midst of the praises of My people. I dwell there because I am happiest there, and just as surely as ye make Me happy with your praising, ye shall make the enemy most unhappy. He has no power whatsoever over a praising Christian. He cannot stand against a praising Church. This is the most powerful weapon ye can use against him. So praise is like a two-edged sword, the one side bringing health to your own spirit and the other side cutting down the enemy.

Open Thine Heart to Me

O My child, I need you for Myself. Yea, I have purposes for thy life beyond thy present comprehension. Yea, I have truth concerning Myself to give to thee deeper and richer and more wonderful than thine understanding has thus far taken in.

Open thine heart wide to Me. I will fill thee with My Holy Spirit, and in so doing will satisfy the deepest longings of thy soul.

Fortitude

In a multitude of testings, thou shalt learn courage. It matters not the price ye pay, but at any cost ye must obtain strength of character and the fortitude to endure. I would build thy resources until ye be able to carry unusually heavy loads and withstand intense pressures.

Ye shall thus become an ambassador of the Kingdom of Heaven to whom I can assign critical missions, being confident that ye are equipped to fulfill them.

It shall be in vain if ye anticipate resting in a comfortable place. Lo, Zion is already filled with those who are at ease. No, ye shall find thyself put in a place of training and discipline, so that when the moments of crisis come ye shall not become faint-hearted, and ye shall not be the victim of unwonted fear.

Trust My instruction in all of this, as ye have in different types of past experiences. I am faithful and loving, and I am doing this in order that ye may meet the future days, and not be found wanting.

On Doing The Father's Work

Behold, I say unto thee, there is a day coming when ye shall regret thy lethargy and ye shall say, 'Why have we left the vineyard of the Lord uncared for?' That with which ye have been occupied shall appear to thee in that day for what it is — chaff and worthlessness. For there shall be nothing of lasting value, and no reward for the works of thine hands, which ye have done in your own strength, and which I have not commanded thee to do.

Jesus Himself was directed by the Father in all that He said and did. Dare ye live according to the dictates of thine own carnal heart and puny human understanding?

Lo, I have fashioned thee for better things. Fail Me not, but place thy life under My divine control, and learn to live in the full blessing of My highest will.

I will strengthen thee and comfort thee and will lead thee by the hand.

LISTEN TO THE SILENCE

". . . no word from God shall be without power. . ."
Luke 1:37 *Ampl. N.T.*

Contents

Find Solitude 135

Be My Ally 136

Stay Pliable In My Hand 137

I Must Have Overcomers 138

Renew Thy Vows 139

The Road Is Steep 141

I Will Use, But Not Destroy You 142

Keep Thy Channel Clear 143

Speak the Truth 144

Come Away, My Beloved 145

Take the Glory With Thee 146

Listen to the Silence 148

A More Glorious Way 149

I Want to Do a Beautiful Work 150

The Secret of Silence 151

The Love Covenant 152

Ye Shall Move Swiftly 154

The Gift of Forgiveness 155

The Eye of the Spirit 157

My Kingdom Is at Hand 158

With Winged Feet 160

Find Solitude

There is no blessing I would withhold from them that walk in obedience to Me — who follow when I call, and who respond when I speak unto them. They are near to my heart and precious in My sight who have eyes to discern My purpose and ears that listen to My direction.

Be not intent upon great accomplishments. By what standards do ye judge the importance of a matter? It was a relatively small thing that Hannah prayed for a son, but what great things I accomplished through Samuel! It may have seemed incidental that Simeon and Anna perceived the Christchild and prophesied over Him; but it was to Me a word worthy to be recorded in Holy Scripture and preserved forever.

Nay, ye cannot ascertain the ways of God amidst the pathways of men. Ye may feel the wind as I pass, and yet see only the swirling dust. The earthly beclouds the heavenly. The voices of men drown the voice of God. Only in much solitude can ye begin to sift away the chaff and come at last to the golden grains of truth.

The World will confuse thee. Silence will speak more to thee in a day than the world of voices can teach thee in a lifetime. Find it. Find solitude — and having discovered her riches, bind her to thy heart.

Be My Ally

My children, do not fear nor resist My voice. When I speak to Thee, ye shall know that it is I, the Lord God. Yea, even as I spake unto Isaiah shall I speak unto thee. Is it not strange that ye should be astonished at the way I speak unto thee? Rather, they ought to marvel who do NOT hear My voice!

Let them not distress thee who doubt the way I deal with thee. Pray rather that the same blessed privilege shall be granted unto them: that their ears be unstopped, and their spirits become sensitive and receptive to the ministering of My Holy Spirit. Pray they may be given a hunger and a burning desire to fellowship more closely with Me.

Surely there is no soul-food nor heart's ease in an intellectual religion, in outward forms and fleshly service. These, while not evil in themselves, are to the soul even as the Bible declares, but filthy rags; and this is no fit nourishment upon which the soul may feed.

When I promised thee green pastures, I had not in mind religious activity. When I said 'Come, buy milk and honey without money nor price', I was not challenging thee to fevered service, but to contemplative fellowship and collective communion. Only thus are souls made strong, and hearts made pure, and minds refreshed.

Thy busyness wearies Me. Small wonder thou art thyself fatigued! Thy fretfulness grieveth Me. I long to take it from thee and give instead the balm of Gilead. BE MY ALLY. I will endue thee with life so dynamic that ye will serve Me before ye even have time to think to put forth the effort to do so. . . .

Stay Pliable In My Hand

O My child, be quick to obey. For the moving of My Spirit may at times be inconvenient to the flesh, and may at other times be diametrically opposed to reason, but obey Me regardless of the cost. Thou wilt in every case be amply repaid for any sacrifice by an abundance of blessing. The more difficult the assignment, the richer the reward.

I will not force thee to make the choice, neither make My will inescapable. There will always be an easier way open to thee, and one seeming to thy mind more reasonable, and involving less risk. In the risk involved, I have calculated to test and develop thy faith as well as thine obedience, and in the choosing process, I give thee an opportunity to prove thy love for Me.

Be sensitive to My Spirit. Be listening for My voice. I will guide thee with My hand upon thy shoulder. I do not intend to circumscribe thy way nor to handicap thy freedom, but rather to lead thee into an increasingly abundant life, and by crucifying the wills of the flesh, to liberate thy spirit.

STAY PLIABLE IN MY HAND, neither resist Me nor be unaware of My working, nor question Me as to what I am making. Trustingly give Me a free hand. It will be a surprise and a joy when the end is revealed.

I Must Have Overcomers

O My children, there is a way that I would lead thee that is not easy for the flesh to bear. It is not a pleasant way, nor in accord with the desires of the carnal nature. I have not purposed to please the self-life, but rather to bring it to the crucifixion; for it can never be a help, but only a hindrance to thy spiritual progress, and to My working through thee.

Ye have faith in Me, this is good, but faith without works is dead. Faith I can give thee as a gift, but the works I can do through thee only as your own ego is moved out of the way. For they are not your works, but My works, even as Jesus said 'I must work the works of Him that sent Me'. And as Paul said 'The life that I now live in the flesh, I live by the faith of the Son of God who loved me and gave His life for me'. And again in another place it is written, 'It is no more I that live, but Christ liveth in Me.'

I will cause the tears to flow through thee in a flood, and I will purge out thy self-life, and I will give thee My love; and with My love, I will give thee My power, and ye shall walk no more in your own way, but ye shall reign with Me in the throne life.

FOR I MUST HAVE OVERCOMERS THROUGH WHICH I MAY OVERCOME. There is an enemy to be contested and defeated; and to do this, there must be more than resolve in thy heart, *there must be power*. This power cannot operate until self-will is put out of the way. Yea, My new life shall become thine in direct proportion to the amount of thy self-emptying.

This I know ye cannot do for thyself; but ye must will it to be done, and as ye will it, I will work with thee and in thee to bring it to pass. Ye shall know joy as never before, and as never possible any other way. Ye shall have rest from inner conflict; yea, ye must be delivered of the inner conflict in order to engage in this outer conflict with the enemy.

Renew Thy Vows

There is a day coming when ye shall say 'I have waited in vain for the Lord'. Lo, ye shall wait for Me to speak, and ye shall hear only the whistling of the wind. For I say unto thee, I am never silent: ye are deaf. I am always speaking; but I find not thine ear attuned to listen.

Ye shall sit alone in a desolate place and grieve in thy loneliness; but it shall not be that I have left thee, but ye have become insensitive to My presence. Yea, I say unto thee, that if ye ignore My personal nearness and fellowship and if ye return not My overtures, ye shall become dull of perception and shall not be able to discern Me even though I am near at hand — even though My love for thee is still as strong as before.

Lo, I say unto thee: Be not lukewarm, lest ye be among those who are cast out of My fellowship. 'How shall ye escape', it is written, 'if ye neglect so great salvation?' But I say now unto thee: How shall ye survive in thy private walk in the Spirit if ye pay but faint heed to My personal nearness to thee and if ye respond not in like kind to the affection I proffer thee?

Thou shalt not be able to meet the needs of others with anything short of this. There is no cure for the ills of humankind but what is contained in the love of God. Ye cannot give to them until after ye have taken it from Me.

'I will not leave you comfortless'. (Jno. 14:18) It is the purpose of My heart to fellowship with thee closely. I am turned away by thy unresponsiveness; by thy preoccupation with things and with people; by thy thoughtlessness and indifference.

Some have lost Me by the sin of rebellion; but I warn thee that ye may lose Me by the subtle way of simple inattention. Confess thy coldness, and draw near to me; and I will make My personal presence real to thee again. I will hold thee close to My heart, and I will let thee hear My voice.

RENEW THY VOWS, and I will revive thy ministry. There is a life ahead for thee into which ye could not have entered before. There is a work ready for thee, and I have prepared thee for it. It is too wonderful to miss. It shall be silent but powerful.

I shall cause the veil to drop, and ye shall enter a new area of experience. Ye shall be given a knowledge in My Spirit that is not to be found in books. I shall share with thee My thoughts, and who can tell the sum of them? Ye shall partake of the Mind of Christ and of the Holy Spirit of God. His eyes go throughout the whole earth seeking out the thoughts and intents of the hearts of men.

Ye shall serve Me in ways ye have never heard of before. It is *My* work. I have laid it out for thee. Keep clear of man's work. Stay free to do Mine. Ye shall not miss it if ye keep close to Me and stay sensitive to My Spirit.

No one else can do what I have reserved for you; and be very sure that if ye fail, it shall remain undone. Crucify the flesh, and let the Spirit thrive. Redeem the time, for surely these days abound with evil.

Bless Me. I will bless you.

The Road Is Steep

Ye are a chosen vessel unto Me, saith the Lord; be not filled with filthy lucre. Be not defiled with the lusts of the flesh and tarnished with the pride of life. Be ye wholesome, humble, simple; for simplicity and a spirit of humility befit one who is a servant of the Lord.

Pride lifteth up. It exalteth self rather than Christ. Humility bringeth down to the level of service, and ye are not to be worshipped, but to serve.

Ye are My treasure. I delight in you when, and only when, ye are fully yielded to Me with no thoughts of personal ambition or achievement. If ye wish for anything, wish for more of My personal nearness. If ye long after anything, long after more of My righteousness and more of My love. For I will not occupy second place, and My Spirit will take leave of an impure vessel. Even as sin hath no place in heaven, just so, I will not dwell in peace in a heart that harbors evil.

So I say unto thee: Put away from thee all that defileth, even as ye would cast away an unclean, evil-smelling, filthy rag. Teach others also how to maintain mental wholesomeness, and how to experience inner cleansing through confession and repudiation of all that offends the Holy Spirit.

Tolerate nothing that dulls the perception of My presence. Cut off, purge out, plead the blood, use every avenue available to thee to rid thy soul of sin. Be never satisfied with half-measures. Be never deterred by satisfaction with the progress already achieved. Know that this is only a beginning.

Holiness is arrived at by no low road. The road to holiness is narrow and steep and exceedingly lonely. There is no other road. "It is the way the Master went, Shall not His servants tread it still?"

I Will Use, But Not Destroy You

O My child, be not overcharged with the cares of everyday living, and let not thine energies be consumed by the humdrum tasks. Such as is needful, ye must do, but if ye put the ministry of the Kingdom in first place, My strength shall be yours for the other tasks, and time shall be given thee for both.

Ye do not need to respond to every call. Learn to discern when I would use you, and when I would have the other individual lean wholly upon Me. Otherwise, ye may restrict the development of the other person's spiritual ministry, and rather than helping, may become an actual hindrance.

I will not over-tax you. I WILL USE YOU, BUT I WOULD NOT DESTOY YOU IN THE USING. But ye may destroy thyself if ye lack this discernment and fail to know when to direct others to look to Me. Ye fear to fail Me. Ye can perhaps fail Me more by an attempt to help another than by refusal, if and when by refusal ye may encourage the other one to seek My face — My help — My instruction.

Ye are also ever in danger of giving incorrect information. Ye may confuse rather than clarify the issue. Be not used by others as a source of information, but challenge these others to seek for light from the same source as you yourself have received it. Be not to them a substitute for My Word — either written, or by prophetic message. Let the question be used as a challenge to Bible study and prayer, and be very reluctant to become the transmitter of quick learning. To be such, poses innumerable disadvantages both for thyself and for the person seeking help. Teach him how to establish communication personally with his God, so that he himself may 'hear from heaven': this is the greatest blessing ye can ever be to another human being.

To be sought after for wisdom is flattering to the ego. Recognize this snare, and be on your guard against it, and bring the flesh to quick crucifixion. Be not as a substitute for God to any man. Be a channel for the ministries of My Spirit, but be never a free giver of advice. Curb the impulse. Give to the other the source of thy knowledge — even the scripture passage where the answer may be found — so that My Word is constantly the first and the final authority.

I will honor My Word, and I will honor them that give to My Word the sacred preeminence which it deserves. My Word shall never return void. It shall accomplish My purposes.

(Isa. 55:11)

Keep Thy Channel Clear

O My daughter, shall I speak unto thee as one whose voice is lost in the noise of crashing surf, or as one who calls in vain in the midst of a deep forest, where there is no ear to hear nor voice to respond? Will ye be as an instrument with broken strings from which the musician can bring forth no music?

Nay, I would have you to be as the waterfall whose sound is continuous, and as a great river whose flow is not interrupted. Ye shall not sing for a time and then be silent for a season. Ye shall not praise for a day, and then revert to the current topics of everyday life.

Ye shall never exhaust My supply. The more ye give, the more will be given unto thee. Ye are in a learning process. I have much to share with thee; yea, out of the abundance of My heart would I instruct thee. I would teach you truths of heavenly wisdom which ye cannot learn from the lips of man. I will instruct thee in the way that thou shalt go. From whom else can ye inquire?

I will bring My love and My life to thee. From whence have ye any such comfort and strength elsewhere? The more often ye come to Me to draw of this water of Life, the more shall thy life be enriched in wisdom — yes, but also in many other ways. Ye have need of My grace that ye may share My truth with a right spirit. Ye need to keep thy channel straight and clear, that My blessing be not hindered in flowing through thee, and that the waters may be kept pure.

Ye do not indicate presumption by continually seeking My face. Ye show, rather, a tendency to trust in the strength of the flesh when ye come *not* to Me for a gift. (Or have ye mistakenly thought that thine own mind had become a source of wisdom?)

Beware of the snare of flattery, and even of well-intended praise. Take not to thyself any glory, nor compliment thyself in thine achievement. I control the waters. I gathered them up in my fist to allow the passage of the children of Israel. I flung them forth to drown the Egyptian army. I send forth the river of life now to refresh and bring life to those who thirst after Me. I dry up the streams of inspiration before the feet of the proud. They shall not drink, saith the Lord, who glory in their own thoughts. They shall be as a desert who pursue the paths of human reason.

Lo, I am not to be found there — even as I was not found in the wind nor in the earthquake. These were natural forces. I was in the still small voice. I Myself am the direct source and the only source of eternal life. Every other well is dry. Every other pursuit is vain.

But ye shall be a fountain flowing forth whose streams shall not fail, for I, the Lord thy God, dwell in the midst of thee.

Speak The Truth

Lo, I say unto thee, be not intimidated by anyone, but speak forth My Word, even as I give it unto thee. Ye have written freely and fearlessly. Now speak in the same way. Thy spoken word must be brought into conformity with the work I have done within thee. This ye need for your own personal sense of unity. This ye need for your own strength. For the house divided against itself cannot stand; neither can ye so long as ye bear one testimony in thine heart and another with thy lips.

Thou art not pleasing Me, but trying to please men. They will detect the inconsistency in spite of your best efforts, for in one way or another, the truth will break through. Ye need not say all that is in thy heart, but ye must either speak the truth or be silent. If ye cannot bring yourself to speak the truth without apology, then speak nothing.

Let the life and witness of Jesus Christ be your guide. If ye are willing to attempt to emulate His honesty, I will come to your aid to give you the wisdom also; so that the answer may be not only true, but forceful. For ye wrestle not against flesh and blood, but against the unseen opposition of satanic forces. These may at times be arrayed against thy soul even through thy dearest friends, so that ye may have to reply as Jesus did to Peter on one occasion.

(Mk. 8:33)

Set not out upon a mission to convert the world to your convictions, but rather to hold your own convictions inviolable against the forces of the opposition. I will be with thee, and will keep thy mouth. Trust Me.

Come Away, My Beloved

O My beloved, ye do not need to make your path (like a snow plow), for lo, I say unto thee, I go before you. Yea, I shall engineer circumstances on thy behalf. I am thy husband, and I will protect thee and care for thee, and make full provision for thee.

I know thy need, and I am concerned for thee: for thy peace, for thy health, for thy strength. I cannot use a tired body, and ye need to take time to renew thine energies, both spiritual and physical. I am the God of Battle, but I am also the One who said: They that wait upon the Lord shall renew their strength. And Jesus said, Come ye apart and rest a little while.

I will teach you, even as I taught Moses on the back side of the desert, and as I taught Paul in Arabia. So will I teach you. Thus it shall be a constructive period, and not in any sense wasted time. But as the summer course to the school teacher, it is vital to thee in order that ye be fully qualified for your ministry.

There is no virtue in activity as such — neither in inactivity. I minister to thee in solitude that ye may minister of Me to others as a spontaneous overflow of our communion. *Never* labor to serve, nor force opportunities. Set thy heart to be at peace and to sit at My feet. Learn to be ready, but not to be anxious. Learn to say 'no' to the demands of men and to say 'yes' to the call of the Spirit. These may sometimes be at variance. Be not distressed by the misunderstanding of people. Let Me take care of them Myself. They too must learn this same important lesson, and thou canst help them by setting the example; but if ye try to please them by answering every demand, ye shall both fall into the same snare.

I am a jealous God, and I am always at peace with Myself. I would have you to be likewise at peace with My Spirit within thee. As ye give Me My rightful place and do not allow others to intrude, ye shall be at peace with Me. Be very serious in this. I am not speaking to thee lightly. I was never more in earnest in any message that I have brought to you. Do not fail Me. I have brought you this message at various times in the past. It was never more urgent than now.

For man is experiencing a new awakening, and he is searching for My Truth more than ever, and I must speak through My prophets; and if they be not separated unto Me, how can I instruct them? Yea, I shall nourish thee by the brook as I nourished Elijah; and I shall speak to thee out of the bush as I spoke to Moses, and reveal My glory on the hillside as I did to the shepherds.

COME AWAY, MY BELOVED, and be as the doe upon the mountains; yea, we shall go down together to the gardens.

Take The Glory With Thee

Behold, I have brought thee out of a dark and solitary land. I have given thee to drink out of My hand. We have held sweet counsel together; for I have not called thee servant, but I have called thee friend. Yea, and I delight in thy companionship. For I have seen thy devotion, and I have observed with pleasure thy thoughtfulness of those less-fortunate ones who have crossed thy path.

For when thou hast encouraged the weary, and when thou hast prayed with the sick, and when thou hast lent help to the needy, comfort to the sorrowing, understanding to the distressed, I count it as unto Myself, for I know that except for thy deep love for Me, thou wouldst not make this kind of sacrifice.

Gifts may be given, prompted by many a selfish motive; but when thou givest thyself, ofttimes in the face of insults, returning good for evil, and in the doing yet receiving further censure; this

I know thou hast done because and only because ye love Me first, and loving Me ye find no place to hate any. For if a man love God, truly he will love his brother likewise. Yea, and he will yet go beyond this, for he will show kindness and feel concern for the needs of even his enemies, and be moved with compassion to minister aid.

Said I not that we must needs go into the valley together? I have given the mountaintop of the enjoyment of My fellowship to prepare thee for the ministry in the valley of service. TAKE THE GLORY OF THE MOUNTAINTOP WITH THEE, yea, My presence, my light, My love. This is not the valley of personal darkness: this is the valley where walk those who need the touch of blessing thou canst bring.

And I am with thee, yea, more so than in any other kind of valley; for in this we are *one* in a very special way. For the Son of Man came to seek and to save that which was lost; to seek that which was lost, and to lift that which was fallen, and to heal that which was bruised.

In this, thy ministry together with Me to those in need, thou 'fillest up that which is left of the sufferings of Christ'. (Col. 1:24) My physical sufferings, the broken body, the shed blood, My death — these were completed at the cross. But the travail of soul until the completion and perfection of the Body of Christ, this continueth until My coming in power and glory to receive unto Myself My chosen Bride.

(For I have chosen each member of the body as an individual, and the Church as a corporate body — so ye are twice-chosen — individually, and collectively.)

So as ye 'pour out thy soul', ye share with Me in My travail until the completion of the purchased possession; until ye all come through the power of the Spirit into the full stature of the Body of Christ, growing up together in Him, each part developing through the nourishment each joint supplieth. (Or, by mutual nurture and encouragement ye stimulate growth each in the other.)

Only as ye yield individually can the work be accomplished. One member in rebellion or hostility retards the growth and injures the health of those about him.

So yield thyself to the movings of the Spirit in thy heart, and minister as I arrange thy contacts, nor set about to make thine own choices. Leave the planning to the Head. This is My work. Let each abide in his place, yielding completely to My Spirit, nourished by My love, and ministering in self-sacrifice.

Listen to the Silence

You are in My hands. You are not keeping yourself; I am keeping you. If I choose to hide you away, it is for a purpose. If I wish to give you a time of rest, it is for thine own good. Nothing is amiss that is in My will. Do not think that it will be as times in the past. I have deeper lessons to teach you. How invaluable have you found the truths to be which I have taught you in your 'Arabia years'. Arabia was not the only solitary period in the life of St. Paul. Indeed, it was rather insignificant in comparison to the later prison day experiences.

One does not write what has already been written. One writes out of the storehouse of fresh revelation and his own personal knowledge gained through the painful experiences of growth. Ye cannot escape the growing experience without forfeiting the other. Ye shall cease writing if ye cease learning. Ye do not learn as ye write, but write as ye learn.

I would spare you if I could do so in love; but this kind of protecting love would be false, and would rob you of much treasure. I only love you truly as I give you My best. My best cannot come to you without pain, even as it could not come to the Lord Jesus without pain. Pain is the result of sin, true, but sin is still an existing problem to be dealt with. It must be grappled with. Empires do not simply fall, but are taken by a stronger force. The kingdom of Satan must likewise be opposed by a stronger force if ye hope to see it fall.

I want to make you strong. I want you to be a Devastator. I have brought you to this place. Make the most of it. Drink in the silence. Seek solitude. LISTEN TO THE SILENCE. It will teach you. It will build strength. Let others share it with you. It is priceless. It is little to be found elsewhere.

A More Glorious Way

Ye have read that the letter killeth but the Spirit giveth life. (2 Cor. 3:6) I say unto thee that I have a deeper revelation of this truth to give unto thee if ye can receive it. For the Spirit operateth in a different realm than the Word. The Word dealeth with thee on the plane of thine everyday living. It governs thy conduct in daily affairs. It guideth thee into the knowledge of the doctrines of God, the understanding of the divine will, and instructs thee in the walk of the Christian.

But in the Spirit, there is a life awaiting thee that would draw thee out beyond the confines of the natural world. The Spirit of God operates in the realm of the supernatural and the infinite.

Do not hold back in wonder and disbelief. Accept My life in the Spirit *as it is*. Do not require Me to operate within the limitations of *thy* life. I am calling *thee* to give My Spirit within thee the liberty to move out into the dimensions of the infinite.

Breath-taking? Yes, perhaps. But how could you expect anything less of Me? Push open the door. In the dazzling light of My presence ye shall see much that now is obscure to thee because of the darkness in which ye have chosen to walk. I have better things for you, — things in keeping with Myself. Ye have not truly known Me. Ye have been hindered in your comprehension by that which ye have read and been taught. There is very little more concerning Me that ye can learn from such human sources. Ye can know Me in the Spirit only as ye go deeper in thy worship. I am not found in textbooks but in sanctuaries. Ye are not changed by knowledge but by love. Only the heart that is melted in devotion is pliable in My hand. Only the mind that is open to the Spirit can receive divine revelation.

Labor not to be wise but to be yielded, and in thine attitude of submission to My Spirit I will instruct thee in My truth. There shall be death and there shall be a glorious resurrection. For the letter shall convict of sin and prune away the old carnal nature, and the Spirit shall bring forth within thee a life that shall never die. It shall have faculties of perception not to be compared with the physical senses; for the mind of the Spirit is the Mind of Christ.

It shall increase and develop as ye move on into God, and ye shall leave behind the graveclothes of religious intellectualism and discover a more glorious way.

I Want to Do a Beautiful Work

Ye are *Mine*, saith the Lord. Ye are not your own. With a very great price have I purchased thee unto Myself. I am not dismayed that ye do not comprehend, but I say unto thee, that if ye will harken unto Me, I will reveal to thee more fully so that ye may know more clearly how vital you are in My purpose. There is work to be done and I need you as a vessel through which to work. Not a vassal, but a vessel. I want to do a beautiful work.

I need an individual to use who is not only available and suitable but who loves Me in such a way as to enhance My creation. I desire not the kind of loyalty a soldier gives to his country, but a dedicated devotion of the type of love more like that which a mother feels toward her unborn child.

There will be inconveniences to be born, self-pleasing to be laid aside, sacrifices and pain, but what a blessed reward I have in store! Yes, in store for *you*, if you are able to let Me use you in the way which I desire to do.

Ye are not unworthy; ye are not unprepared. Ye have no reason to hold back unless it be that your love for Me is too small. If this be the only hindrance, draw closer to Me, and I shall pour My love out upon you and thus shall your own affection for Me be deepened and perfected. Lo, I wait for you. Come to Me.

The Secret of Silence
(Praise and Reproof)

My child, let not the words of others influence thee unduly —either their praise or their criticism. Weigh each for its proper value, and come back to Me again. Only in communion with Me can ye be sure of the truth. If I correct thee, ye know it is for thy betterment. If I encourage thee with a word of praise, it is because I know ye need it; so rejoice in it and accept it as wholeheartedly as ye accept My rebukes.

Ye know My rebukes are for thy benefit. Can ye not believe that My words of commendation are for the same purpose? Some of thy faults and weaknesses can best be helped and corrected by *praise* rather than by *reproof*. When ye turn a deaf ear in an effort to be humble, you are not helping. Ye cannot be truly humble until ye have a deep sense of being loved.

Knowing and truly feeling that such great love is not merited in the face of thy many imperfections will generate more honest humility than a thousand rebukes for obvious failures. Ye are condemned already by thine own heart. There is a subtle pride that seeks to hide these glaring imperfections in the effort to hold some vestige of self-esteem and invoke the respect of others. This is a craftiness of the enemy.

If ye will accept My love and My approval, ye shall be given courage to face thy sins and faults and deal with them with more decisiveness. The more ye find of the truth about thine own self, the more ye shall be set free . . . free of improper evaluations of thy worth and false pride that seeks to cover recognized flaws.

I want your life and character and personality to be as beautiful and lovely as I visualized it to be when I created you. Much has not developed perfectly. Some early beauty has been marred. *Live close to Me*, and let Me re-mold and re-create until I see in thee the image of all I want thee to be.

I love thee, My child — My very dear and special child. Through thy childhood years I walked very close to thee, and in thy childlike way ye were very conscious of My presence and reality. Ye have made an arduous journey. Ye have climbed many a mountain that ye could easily have walked around. Ye have not chosen the pleasant path nor sought joys though they were readily accessible.

Ye have often misconstrued My will and felt that only in sacrifice and suffering could ye please Me, whilst much of the time I have longed to deliver thee out of the very pains ye thus inflicted upon thyself. Ye meant to please Me, but in truth ye were only marring thine own beauty — which is precious to Me.

I cannot rejoice in a blighted rose. Ye have gone far enough in this way. I offer thee *My* path now, if ye are strong enough to accept it. Life and liberty and love and joy. Health and peace — simplicity and rest. It has been there for you all along. You can have it even now if ye will.

I don't want you to work for Me under pressure and tension like a machine — striving to produce, produce. I want you to just LIVE with ME as a PERSON. I have waited for you to wear yourself out. I knew you would find it eventually — the secret of silence and rest, of solitude and of song.

I will rebuild your strength — not to work again in foolish frenzy, but just for the sake of making you strong and well. To Me this is an end in itself. Make it your aim and join with Me wholeheartedly in the project. 'Many joys are waiting yet.'

The Love Covenant

My children, there is no good thing that I would withhold from thee. I have not left you to fend for yourselves nor to make your way by your own devices. I am the Lord, thy God. I am thy provider and thy defender. I care for thee with a deep and tender love. I am all-wise and all-powerful, and will be thy defense against every onslaught of the enemy.

Anticipate My help. I will not fail thee. Look down at the path before thee. Thou shalt see the print of My feet, for as scripture saith, I go before thee, and I make the path ready for thee as ye follow.

152

It is a joy to My heart when My children rely upon Me. I delight in working things out for thee, but I delight even more in *thee thyself* than in anything I do to help thee. Even so, I want *you* to delight in *Me* just for *Myself*, rather than in anything ye do for Me.

Service is the salvage of love. It is like the twelve baskets of bread that were left over. The bread partaken of was like fellowship mutually given; and the excess and overflow was a symbol of service. I do not expect thee to give to others until ye have first thyself been a partaker. I will provide you with plentiful supply to GIVE if ye first come to RECEIVE for thine own needs.

This is in no way selfishness. It is the Law of Life. Can the stalk of corn produce the ear unless first it receive its own life from the parent seed? No more can ye produce fruit in thy ministry except ye be impregnated with divine life from its source in God Himself. It was from the hands of the Christ that the multitudes received bread. From His hands ye also must receive thy nurture, the Bread of Life to sustain thy health and thy life.

THIS IS HIS LOVE-COVENANT WITH YOU. It is the message of John 15. Abide in Me, for the branch cannot bear fruit except it abide in the vine. No more can ye except ye abide in Me. This abiding is a love relationship, and this is why I said 'Service is the salvage of love'.

Service will be futile and burdensome unless it springs from an overflowing heart. Overflowing not with good intentions and condescending self-righteousness, but overflowing with the love of God. This ye do not have of thyself, nor can ye give, however much ye might desire to do so. Ye shall possess *this love* only as ye wait upon Me and take time to absorb it from Me, even as a quiet flower takes life from the warm rays of the sun.

Thy heart shall be cold otherwise. For thy ready ardor and natural sympathy and common kindness shall be soon cooled by the chill winds of ingratitude and other unlovely reactions of other people. Think ye the love of Jesus was always well-received? Would He not have brought His ministry to an abrupt end on many an occasion if He had needed appreciation of people to motivate His loving service?

Have ye read the reaction of the religionists to the recital of His miracle-working power in Luke 4? The exhibition of God's love draws forth emotions in the unregenerate heart that are nothing short of murderous at times. In other cases, they are met by callous indifference and criminal ingratitude, as with the nine lepers who never returned to express so much as a word of thanks for their deliverance from a walking death.

In the face of divine love being poured forth on Calvary — the holy, sinless God Himself dying for sinful, depraved, undeserving man; what is the reaction? Gratitude? Love responding? Contrition? No! Hate lashing out in jeers and mocking. Violence and cruelty flowing forth like a river and mingling with the very blood that was spilt for their redemption!

No. Human kindness will never be enough. It will never fill the twelve baskets with fragments. There will never be any crumbs left over for others except first ye be partaker in your own personal love feast with the Saviour.

Let Him fully satisfy thy soul-hunger, and *then* thou shalt go forth with a full basket on thine arm. Twelve baskets there were. (Matt. 14:20) One for each disciple. There will always be the multitudes to be fed, but the few called to minister. This is by My own arrangement. As the scripture says: Do not many desire to be teachers, for thereby is attached more heavy responsibility. (James 3:1)

Many are the called. Few are the chosen.

Ye Shall Move Swiftly

Behold, out of gross darkness, a light shall shine forth. Yea, out of the night shall a cry be heard. For I will make known My will unto thee, and thou shalt go no more halting, but YE SHALL MOVE SWIFTLY AND SURELY. Thou mayest not know what I am doing as yet, but ye shall know hereafter, and ye shall be moved by My divine unction and authority.

Ye shall not be left to falter as the blind searcheth out his way; but thou shalt put thine hand into Mine and we shall move out together. My Spirit shall be clothed upon by thy life and testimony, and thou shalt be empowered by My might and power.

My strength is indefatigable. Yea, I will be so to thee — I will be an energizing and a quickening power within thee and upon thee, and thou shalt go in the strength of thy God. Thou shalt not fail; neither shall thine arm droop nor thy foot lag.

Thou hast no enemy to fear but only fear itself. Thou hast no weakness to contend with but such as doubt may produce. Look unto Me — yea, constantly set thine eyes upon My face, and thou shalt be as the eagle and as the deer. Rest thine heart in Me. For in quietness and in returning shall be thy peace and thy strength.

Be anxious for nothing, but in all situations in prayer and in fastings, bring each emergency case to Me, for I am the Great Physician; and many are the afflictions of the righteous, but the Lord healeth them all.

Blessings and honor and praise and glory be unto Thee forever and ever. Amen.

The Gift of Forgiveness

O My child, come to Me — I want to give you a new gift. I want you to see all people as being under the shed sacrifice of the blood of Christ.

He has died for all. His forgiveness encompasseth all. Tell them. It is the Good News. They will accept it even as they have received eagerly and joyfully the message of My *love*. It is the confidence in thine own heart that will engender faith to receive within the hearts of others.

Freely forgive all, even as ye have freely loved all. Those to whom ye extend My forgiveness shall come to experience it for themselves even as ye would extend a helping hand to lift another across a brook. Having gained the safety of the other side, he needeth thy help no longer but standeth as secure as thyself; but he needed assistance in crossing over.

Be not dull and slow. Many are waiting for the out-stretched hand. Many have hung a black veil of self-condemnation between their own guilty hearts and the light and power of My forgiveness. Thou canst approach them from the other side and reach them with the message where they have no pre-set defense.

They are all around you. Sing it, shout it, speak it patiently and whisper it tenderly. The dead shall rise to life: the hopeless to joy: the desponding to courage: the poor to receive My bounty.

Whosesoever sins ye remit shall be remitted. Those who receive no ministry may never find their way through to the light, knowing not the path. To you has been committed and entrusted the mysteries of the Kingdom. Keep them not stored away in hidden vaults. Scatter them along thy way and place the jewels in the empty hands of those ye encounter on the road of life.

Thou wilt find the Christ Himself standing beside thee, and thou shalt see His smile. Ye may have but a small place in the life of thy brother, but thou shalt have a very special place in the heart of thy Lord. Go forth, then, in faith, giving My forgiveness. Blessing shall attend thee and heaven shall rejoice in thy successes.

I am bringing you into a new ministry. The former shall be enriched and made more full and more meaningful. I am not undoing anything. I am adding to. I shall be enriching thine own soul and effecting thy sanctification.

Ye have need of many graces as well as many gifts. The *graces* of thy soul accompany thee into the next life, whereas the *gifts* are left behind. For this reason the health of thine own soul is of more importance to thyself than the fulness of thy ministry. But each time ye launch out into a new ministry ye bring new life and strength and health-building forces into operation within thine own soul.

The Eye of the Spirit

O My children, I am the door. I am the door of salvation; I am the door of peace and hope. Yea, I am the door of revelation. And even as My written Word is the revelation of the Lord Jesus Christ, even so shall My spoken word be unto thee. It shall be an unveiling before thy very eyes of the person and the work of the Anointed One. For ye shall not be as those who remain unto this day with a veil over their eyes.

Nay, but ye shall be as My servant, the Apostle Paul, who in his baptism experience had the scales fall from his eyes, and what visions were given to him in the Spirit! Ye too shall see. Ye shall SEE, for the Lord thy God shall grant to thee foresight and insight, and ye shall be allowed to look into those things which scripture says are hidden even from the angels.

Ye shall see the coming together of the Body of Christ. Ye shall behold the glory. Ye shall see visions of things to come, and of some ye shall witness the fulfillment. Ye shall be given discernment. Yea, that which is in darkness shall be to thee as though it were exposed to light; yea, that which is hidden shall be revealed to thee. For in the eye of the Spirit there is no darkness, and ye shall see with the eye of the Spirit.

The limitations of thy natural vision shall be no handicap. The Spirit is not detained by the flesh. The Spirit shall move in spite of the flesh, and shall accomplish a renewal and shall do a work of re-creating, so that the newly-liberated creature shall rise up in virgin life, starting out upon a ministry the foundations of which no man has laid. It shall be a path of holiness, a way of miracles, and a life of glory. There shall be the shining of My smile.

Naught shall be required of thee but obedience. Thou shalt follow the call of the Spirit and not search for the path; for the way shall be laid down before thee even as ye tread. Wherever ye stop, there shall the path stop also. Whenever ye walk in faith, the way shall be made clear before thee.

Be as a young child and step out in confidence, knowing that with thy hand in Mine ye shall be always safe and blessings shall attend thee.

My Kingdom Is at Hand

By My Spirit, saith the Lord, shall I speak to My people. They shall sing of My glory who hear My voice. They shall be filled with rejoicing who behold My countenance. They shall bring their offerings of praise, and I shall bless them out of the riches of My heart. The more they bless Me, the more will I honor them. They shall walk in a path of delight who are pure of heart. Joy is the natural climate of heaven, and My chosen ones who delight in Me shall have a full portion even now.

Be prepared for Me, for I shall come unto thee in a blinding splendour, and ye shall not be able to bear it if ye have been regarding the darkness about thee. Look above the present scene, for to dwell on the confusion of the world would unfit thee for the revelation of heaven. You are not going to be here much longer, and no one spends time nor thought on what is soon to be left behind.

Abundantly have I blessed you. Thy gratitude for this is fitting. But there are far more wonderful things that I am about to do for you, so keep thy heart free and thy mind stayed upon Me. The Great Revelation is unfolding, and the ushering in of My Kingdom is at hand. I would prepare thee. I have truth to give thee that is vital to this hour. Ye need to receive it now so that ye shall not be perplexed.

It shall indeed be a dark hour for the world, and humanity shall be enshrouded in a darkness such as in the days of the flood. This shall be an even greater darkness, and there shall be anguish and travail. But out of this shall come a new age — of righteousness and of peace, and all creation shall struggle in travail until it be brought forth.

But I am lifting My chosen ones even now into a realm of glory and revelation. Yea, I am bringing forth a special unique creation. It shall be as Noah and as Lot, even the righteous remnant which shall be delivered out of destruction.

For judgment must fall upon sin and all ungodliness. Evil must be purged and put away. *But I will always have a witness,* saith the Lord, and I will not forsake My people who put their trust in Me. The greater the judgment, the greater the deliverance; and the greater the darkness, the greater the glory. The greater the lie, the greater the Truth.

These are going to be Glorious days for you, My chosen. (And this has been a mutual choosing. If the world would choose Me now, I would usher in My Kingdom now, even as in the days of Jesus' earthly ministry. Israel had then the opportunity to accept her Messiah. Having rejected, judgment ensued. So it is today. Mankind has had nearly two thousand years to accept My grace and My forgiveness and salvation. Having rejected, doom is inevitable.)

This is the night of man's rebellion and disobedience. Ye are beginning to see the fulfillment of the second Psalm. But in this night, the door shall be opened. It shall be opened by the Bridegroom, and they who are watching, and they who have maintained their lamps of witness shall go in. Others shall see and shall desire to enter, but shall be too late.

See that thy witness not cease. Only as ye have a full supply of My Spirit can the fire of testimony be kept alive. They who hold darkened lamps could scarcely be unbelievers; for the lamp is My Word. My Word without My Spirit can produce no witness. The fire is the witness, and the fire cometh never from the Word alone, but always from the Word and the oil of the Spirit. See that ye lose not the oil. When those who possess the oil have been taken away, where shall ye go to buy?

Be filled, My people, and be burning, for when I come I shall come for the living, not for the dead; for the Living Witness I shall preserve to carry the light over into the Kingdom Age.

With Winged Feet

O My children, the time is short. Be not as those who live for the pleasures of the moment; for all that is of the world is earthly. It shall not endure, but shall be as chaff carried away by the wind. I am aware of thy needs and shall provide in abundance, but it is for My glory and My honor, and I shall have the praise.

Thou shalt tread lightly and not allow thy feet to be ensnared in the net of undue concern for the things about thee. They are Mine, saith the Lord, even as all things are Mine, and you yourselves are Mine; and I am more interested in you than in things. Likewise, I want you to be occupied with Me rather than with My gifts. I will take care of both them and thyself. Is it not a small thing for me to do?

Be alert to My voice. Let not thine ear lose its keenness of listening. Be devoted to Me with thy whole heart, and put all that is about thee into My keeping. For I have not many to whom I can speak as I have spoken to thee. Ye shall be My mouthpiece in places where there are no other voices to be heard.

Ye shall magnify My Name in a dark corner. Thou shalt praise Me in a place where others extol men. Thou shalt evidence My love and reality to those who have not as yet experienced My nearness and fellowship in the way in which you have known Me.

I have need of thee as a light to shine in dark places. I have not called thee by some fickle whim. As it is written, How shall the message go out without a messenger? I have made thee My messenger. Thou shalt go with winged feet. Thou shalt not allow thy foot to be bogged down in the mire of earthly cares and riches.

Thou shalt discharge thy duties with dispatch and shalt deal in wisdom with each responsibility; but thine heart shall rest in My hand. Thy thoughts shall return to Me as the needle to the pole and as the bird to its nest. (Even as the bird that returns after migration.)

SOUNDING OF THE TRUMPET

"And every man that hath this hope in him purified himself, even as he is pure."

I John 3:3

Contents

The Secret (poem).. 167

Delight Thyself in Me.. 168

Relinquish Thy Will.. 169

With the Strong Cords of My Faithfulness.. 170

In Love I Chasten.. 171

I Control the Winds.. 172

Allow Me Ingress to Thy Heart.. 173

Come Into the Secret Chambers of Communion...................................... 174

I Seek to Lift Thy Load.. 174

Heart-Purity 175

Thy Life Is as a Weaving.. 176

I Wait for Thee.. 177

Enter the Flow.. 178

I Make No Provision for the Laggard.. 180

The Solitary Relationship.. 181

Relax Not Thy Vigil.. 182

According to Mine Eternal Purposes.. 183

These Are Days of the Moving of My Spirit.. 183

Give Not Substitutes.. 184

Stay Beneath My Wing.. 185

Bread Upon the Waters.. 186

The Master Artist.. 187

I Am Bringing Sons Into Glory.. 188

Shout the Victory.. 188

As the Sounding of the Trumpet.. 189

Ye Shall Come Forth as Gold.. 190

I Shall Come Singing.. 191

Expect the Unexpected 192

Eternal Destiny of the Present Moment 192

The Secret

There's a little word that changes
    Darkest skies to brightest blue;
There's a little word that brings the
    Sunlight bravely shining through.
Never mind the things about you;
    Never mind if others frown—
Lift your face to God and praise Him,
    And the blessings will come down!

Praise is mightier than an army
    With its banners all unfurled;
Praise will win the victory sooner
    Than all the powers of this world.
For the God who ruleth all things,
    And the God who longs to bless
Waiteth only till He heareth thee
    Thy love to Him confess.

Beg Him not for any blessing;
    Tire Him not to spell thy need.
This He knoweth e'er thou speak it;
    Stay Him not to beg and plead.
Lift thy face and sing it heav'nward,
    From the deeps within thy soul;
Let His praises fill thy being,
    Let the shout of rapture roll.

Ah! the rest will come quite easy—
    E'er thou thinkest, 'twill be done.
Thou wilt know PRAISE is the answer.
    Thou wilt find the vict'ry won.
Blessed, holy, wondrous Jesus,
    Heav'n in Thee to me is come!

Delight Thyself in Me

My child, be not anxious concerning the growth of thy soul. Leave it with Me. Have I not said that the lilies grow without taking thought of themselves? Even so must ye, both in the natural and in the spiritual.

To be sure, there are conditions that must be met in order to insure healthy, normal development; however, these conditions are not created by anxiety, but anxiety militates against them.

Be occupied with acquainting thyself with My character and My person. Revel in My fellowship. Thy very association with Me, if it be sufficiently consistent, will bring about changes in thine own personality that will be a surprise to thee when discovered, even as thou hast so often experienced the joy of finding a new bloom on a cherished plant.

Turn thy face toward Me, and leave to Me the responsibility of probing thy soul. I am the Master Surgeon. I am skilled in all the cures of the soul as well as those of the body. Let Me care for thy health.

Delight thyself in Me, and I shall bring about that which ye desire to see in thy character and personality. Feed upon My Word. It is there that ye shall come to a clearer understanding of My Person. Only as ye know Me can ye come to be more like Me.

In association with others, man taketh to himself a measure of the mannerisms and ideologies of these other persons. So shall it be likewise to those who spend much time in My company.

Silently, and without conscious effort, thou shalt be changed.

Relinquish Thy Will

Ho, every one that thirsteth, come ye to the waters, and he that hath no money; come ye, buy, and eat; yea, come buy wine and milk without money and without price. Isaiah 55:1

Lo, My heart is grieved by thine independence. How would Joseph have felt if his father and family had remained at home, starving in the famine, when he had invited them to share the bountiful stores which he had at his disposal and desired to share freely with them? (Ge. 45)

Would he not have grieved far more deeply than over the unjust actions of his brothers who hated him? For to be rebuffed by a loved one causeth pain not to be compared with the cruelties inflicted by an enemy. So thine indifference and unresponsiveness to My call bringeth anguish to My soul, yea, deeper grief than the crimes of the reprobate sinner. For My rod have I laid upon the sinner, but Mine hand have I laid upon thee.

And I have put Mine arm about thee to draw thee closer, but ye have been impatient and irritable as though I sought to interfere with thy liberty. Lo, I am able to give thee greater liberty than thou shalt ever find by seeking to be independent of Me. I seek not to interfere with thy happiness, but I do require that thou relinquish thy will; for I cannot bless thee as I desire to do until thy will is yielded up and thou accept Mine in exchange.

As thou lovest Me, thou acceptest My will as thine own, and the calibre and extent of thy love for Me may be accurately measured by the degree to which thou hast accepted My will with a peaceful heart.

Thou canst best sing 'My Jesus I love Thee' when thou canst truly sing 'Where He Leads Me, I Will Follow' . . . And I say unto thee, that he that taketh not up his cross daily to follow Me cannot be My disciple.

With the Strong Cords of My Faithfulness

O My child, I have loved thee with an everlasting love.

With the strong cords of My faithfulness have I bound
Myself to thee.

Throughout all the days of thy sojourn, I have been deeply
concerned for thee,

nor turned I My attention from thee at any time.

Darkness may have pressed about thy soul, but I was near at hand.

The night of affliction may obscure thy vision,
but the night and the day are both alike to Me.

When thou passeth through the waters, I am with thee.

Whether thou seest Me or not, I am at thy side.

Though at times thou feelest only aloneness,
yet Mine hand is upon thee,

yea, Mine arm doth encircle thee, and Mine heart is touched
by thy grief.

I suffered in all ways as ye suffer, but ye shall never suffer
as I suffered;

for I experienced one awful moment of separation from
the Father;

but I have promised that I will NEVER forsake thee,
and I will never leave thee.

In Love I Chasten

Behold, I am the Lord thy God, the Eternal, the Almighty. The Alpha and the Omega, the Beginning and the Ending — the Great Unchanging One, yea, the Bright and Morning Star, that lighteth every one that cometh into the world. And My light hath not grown dim, but it increaseth more and more in its intensity as the day approacheth: the great and terrible day of judgment when all men's hearts shall be laid open to the scrutiny of the light of My truth.

For My Truth abideth ever, and no man shall escape, for it shall be as a flaming sword as it proceedeth out of My mouth, and every mouth shall be stopped. For in judgment shall I come, to purge the world and to set up My Kingdom.

But I have sent My Holy Spirit into your hearts *now* that He might judge your hearts daily, so that ye may be accounted worthy to escape the day of wrath. For if ye walk now in the light of My revealed truth and if ye judge yourselves, ye shall not be judged at that coming day. And if thou shalt allow the searching eye of the Holy Spirit to find thee out, then it shall not be said to thee, 'thy sins shall find thee out.'

Resist Me not and harden not your hearts. Provoke Me not to use My chastening rod, for I love thee. I would not drive thee with a whip, nor bridle thee with rein and bit to prevent thee from plunging into error; but only let Me look into thine eyes, and I will guide thee in love and gentleness.

I take no pleasure in the affliction of My children. In love I chasten to prevent the deeper suffering that would be involved if I allowed thee to go on in a path of evil. But My heart is glad when thou walkest close, with thy hand in Mine, and we may talk over the plans for each day's journey and activities — work and pleasures — so that it becometh a happy way that we travel in mutual fellowship.

So pour out thy praise to Me from a light heart. I will plan thy path and we shall go singing. No cloud shall mar. No storm shall break.

Praise God! — He not only knoweth the way that I take, but He will walk it with me, and I shall find comfort in His companionship.

I Control the Winds

My child, be not dismayed by any calamity that befalleth thee. Thy times are in My hand. Thy way is open before Me, and I have all in My control. Never doubt My care. Never question My dealings.

Ye shall know that I am leading thee by the narrowness of the way. Yea, it is ofttimes a difficult and a precipitous path; but I would assure thee of My hand of protection. Do not think it strange that I bring you by this route, for I say unto thee that there is a raucous crowd on the other road, and there is an abundance of places of entertainment and of places to eat and to drink.

I am not taking you that way, because in the solitary and the steep and narrow way I shall have opportunity to deal with thee and to teach thee; and ye shall be blessed and shall learn to praise Me with uncontrollable joy.

I cannot produce saints and shape My character and image within you by allowing you full and unrestricted liberty. There can be nothing profitable for you in the matter of the growth of thy soul if ye go the way of abandon.

Put thy life in My hands, and it shall be for thee a place of peace and of spiritual comfort. So long as ye abide in this place, I shall control the rains that fall upon thee and the winds that blow. So long as ye are in My hands, ye are in a garrison the walls of which no enemy shall scale.

Allow Me Ingress to Thy Heart

O My people, be watchful and be much in prayer. I cannot mold thee and shape thee and perfect thee unless ye provide Me the opportunity to do so. I can only minister to the needs of thy soul as ye allow Me ingress to the hidden places of thy heart.

Ye can set up a barrier against Me to prevent My entrance, and I will not interfere. Open wide thy being to Me in the intimacy of prayer, and then, and only then, shall I take the liberty to correct thee and show thee thy faults.

I long to do this for thee, because I desire to make thee into a closer resemblance to My divine nature. I would change thy human frailties to My strength. I would take thy resentments, and give thee My grace. I would take thy natural inclination to anger, and give thee My unerring tendency to love and to forgive.

I am thy God, and I rule the universe and keep it operating by My will. But to thee I have given this most sacred thing: *thy will.* I have given thee so much freedom that ye may even exercise that will against Me, if ye choose to do so.

Yield to Me, and I will shape and form thy soul to conform to My pattern of beauty and holiness. Much that is considered as holiness by men's standards is distortion in My eyes. Ye are not prepared to judge thine own life, neither to draw a pattern for piety.

Fix thine heart upon Me, and as ye behold My glory, ye shall be changed, and My own likeness shall be formed within thee.

Come Into the Secret Chambers of Communion

O My beloved, My desire is toward thee. Yea, My heart longeth after thee. Grieve Me not by thine indifference. For I would gather thee; but ye heed Me not. I would embrace thee and caress thee; but ye are impatient to be away. Ye cannot please Me thus.

For I have called thee to come into the secret chambers of solitary communion. They are dark; but the comfort of My Person is there. Out of darkness cometh great treasure.

The dazzle and glitter of public life is attractive to the eye of the carnal man; but I would closet you away in the secret places of humility and discipline of soul, denying the things that pertain to the outward man in order to perfect the inner life and enrich thy knowledge of Myself.

I Seek to Lift Thy Load

Seek Me early; seek Me late; seek Me in the midst of the day. Ye need Me in the early hours for direction and guidance and for My blessing upon thy heart. Ye need Me at the end of the day to commit into My hands the day's happenings — both to free thyself of the burdens and to give them over into My hands that I may continue to work things out. And ye need Me more than ever in the busy hours, in the activities and responsibilities, that I may give thee My grace and My tranquility and My wisdom.

I do not ask you to take time for Me with the intention of placing a burden upon thee in requiring thee to do so. Rather than adding a requirement, I seek to lift thy load. Rather than burdening thee with a devotional obligation, I desire to take from thee the tensions of life.

Heart-Purity

O My children, 'tis not in thy grieving over thy sins that they are forgiven. Lo, I say unto thee that My forgiveness is in constant operation and ye need only accept it. The cleansing of thy heart and the restoration of thy joy depends upon thy full confession and willingness to repent and to renounce thy sin. It is in this area that ye need to exercise thy soul toward the achievement of heart-purity, and until this work is accomplished (and maintained) ye shall not have inner peace.

This unrest and conflict that ye suffer is not caused by My attitude toward thee but by thine attitude toward thyself. Ye know that all is not well within. Ye would do well to seek My face in repentance until all that distresses thee is yielded up to Me.

Much that is truly sin and is causing thee distress is not even recognized by thee as such. Ye are in truth plagued more by these unidentified enemies than by all the overt sins ye have ever committed. For the overt sins are readily recognized and sorely grieved over, and for most of these forgiveness has already been received.

Lo, it is the little foxes that are spoiling the vine. Thy vine hath tender grapes. If ye were bearing no fruit, ye would not be thus molested.

Rejoice in that ye know that the enemy would not trouble thee unless ye were of some value to Me. It was not an evil man that the devil chose to try in Old Testament days, but one of whom it was written that he was perfect before His God. (Job 2:3)

No true saint who seeketh to please Me escapes the onslaughts of the devil. He is a prime target who sets himself to a life of prayer. Ye need the armor if ye decide to go out to battle. For in serving Me, ye anger the enemy and he will not allow thee to gain ground spiritually without seeking to hurl against thee his poisoned arrows of doubts and accusations.

Resist him, as scripture admonishes thee. He is not courageous, but he is sly, and he is not easily discouraged. Ye can never escape his snare until ye recognize his activities and strike at the source.

Do not attack thy discouragement, but resist the one who would put it upon thee. Do not doubt My forgiveness, but close thine ears to the accuser.

Thy Life Is as a Weaving

My child, thy life is as a weaving. Beauty shall not come to thee by joy alone. Life may be tortuous at times, and the pathway rough. From fabrics of lovely silk and from cords of rougher materials, I fashion what pleaseth Me. Ye may never know why certain experiences come. It is enough that My hand brings them all.

My grace is limited in no way by sorrow and difficulty. Indeed, it shines like a strand of gold mixed in with the black of grief. My hand moveth with infinite love and I am creating a pattern of intricate beauty.

Be never dismayed. The end shall bring rejoicing for both thyself and Me. For ye are My workmanship, created in Christ, even in His mind before the worlds existed.

Doubt not, for My will *shall* be done.

He took away the stain of sin
And made me clean and pure within;
He took away the strain of care
And now I find peace everywhere.

I Wait for Thee

Behold, with great love have I chosen thee and made thee Mine, saith the Lord. Yea, My heart is drawn out toward thee, and I would minister to thee.

I wait for thee to turn from everything else to Me alone. I want you to give Me all of yourself. I want the real you. The more you can bring to Me of your true self, the more I can give to you of My true self.

If ye come to Me with any kind of cloak over your soul, just to this extent ye hinder Me from fully opening My heart to you. I am neither disturbed by imperfections nor impressed with piety. People look upon the outward, but I am only concerned with the heart; for I know that whenever I can occupy the heart, all will be working toward perfection in the outer man.

And so I bypass the outer man temporarily, and when I come to you, I come via the very citadel of thy soul — not as an intruder from the outside.

It is as though a guest came to a home and entered the inner sanctum, rather than coming by way of the outer gate. He would then not be mindful of the gate or the garden nor the exterior of the house. I come to thee via My Holy Spirit from depths within thy being that thou hast never plumbed; from chambers within thy soul which thine eyes have never seen. — Rooms of darkness. — Not dark because of sin necessarily, as ye think of sin; but dark because they have been kept closed.

Indeed, none but I have the key to open them. I not only have the power to open them, but the wisdom and the love; and I never confront thee with that which I do not give thee grace to meet.

Enter the Flow

O My child, My child, I love thee. I need thee. I need thee because I love thee. I call thee through the trees. In the soughing of the pines, it is My voice speaking. I call thee in the wind. In the breaking of the waves, it is My voice thou hearest. In the tumbling waters of the brook, it is I, calling, ever calling.

Go not forth out of thy house with a closed ear. Walk not in a garden with inattentive soul. Pluck not a flower except with thy heart athrob.

Learning, knowing, working, these all have their place. But these are not the core of life; for living at its center is loving, else it is not life. Work becometh the fabric from which we weave life only when love holdeth the threads. Knowledge enricheth life to the degree that love controlleth the thinking. Pleasure becometh the path to the far country if true love has been left behind in pursuit of false values.

Learn to love Me and to love Me well. Let the voice within thee answer the voice without. Be at one with the trees, with the waves, with the flowing brook. Grow upward, as trees, and seek My face. Dwell deep, as the lake, and know My fulness and quiet. And move ever, always, determinately onward, as the brook, and keep the outflow of thy life ever in motion.

For in My speaking, thou shalt gain insight. In My stillness, thou shalt gain poise; and joining with Me in the flow, thou shalt experience the progressive life. Yea, only as life is progressive is it life at all. Movement indicates life. Movement safeguards life. Movement promulgates life. Movement giveth purpose to life — yea, beauty.

It is the flowing lines of the sculptor's work that spell success. It is the flowing movement of the musical score that transforms mere notes to true song. It is the ministries of mother to child, either physical or spiritual, that contribute to the formation of the new personality and character. It is in the fulfillment of the joint responsibilities and services between husband and wife that love is nurtured and fulfillment experienced.

It is love *being* and love *doing*. Yea, it is love *loving*. Otherwise it is concept, not reality. It is the believer *worshipping* — otherwise it is empty religion, with all spiritual creativity lost, and if not found in time, destroyed.

So the trees would say to thee, *Speak*. Speak to Me, speak of Me — for I am always speaking.

And the lake would say to thee, *Be still*. Be still before Me in communion, and be still at times even in the company of others, that ye may enjoy the lesson of the lake in mutual fellowship.

And *Move*. Find the channel of creativity within thy soul. I have made no man without it. Some have choked it with indifference; others have despised it in rebellion; others have ignored it in foolishness; others have twisted it in bitterness. But I stand ready to come to the assistance of any man or woman who sincerely endeavors to find his channel, to remove debris, to repair damage or straighten the course, and most of all to enter the flow.

It is the flow of divine life. Dam it off by self-centeredness, and it becometh a dead sea. Labor, learn, attempt to live apart from its power and impetus, and all is ultimately weariness of body, frustration of soul, disappointment of heart and failure in purpose.

Come unto Me all ye that labor and are heavy laden; enter the stream of My life and ye shall find rest, ye shall find power, ye shall find overflowing joy, ye shall discover with delight that ye have truly become partaker of My life, co-laborer in My Father's work, and recipient of inestimable rewards.

I Make No Provision for the Laggard

I am in the midst of thee, My children. Ye have heard My voice and have known that it is I Myself who have been ministering unto thee. Ye have not followed the voice of a stranger nor sought out strange paths. For this reason have I set My love upon thee. I have put Mine arm around thee, and with My wings have I sheltered thee. Ye are the object of My special attention and ye have received My special care.

I have given thee of My best because ye have loved Me. I have drawn thee into My banqueting hall because ye have hungered and thirsted after the things of God. Yea, because ye have longed for righteousness and true holiness I have sought thee out to instruct thee and teach thee in My laws and in My ways. I will indeed bring thee to a higher realm of experience and revelation because there is a quest in thy soul after Truth.

The Word is verily near thee, even in thine heart. Listen to the voice of My Spirit within. It will never fail. It will never be silent. It will never mock thy cry. Thine hours of meditation shall be rich in the treasures of thy God, and His light shall guide thee.

It is no futile path in which I am leading you. It shall be laden with blessing and filled with surprises. Be not hesitant to follow. If ye lag behind, ye may find My footprints have become cold because I have gone on too far ahead. I charge you to keep pace with Me. I will not gauge My steps too wide for thee to follow. I will measure them to thine ability, but I make no provision for the laggard.

Follow close, and your reward shall be blessed.

The Solitary Relationship

Praise Me out of the fulness of thy heart. Out of the depths of thy soul let thy songs arise. For the Lord hath dealt bountifully with thee; yea, He hath blessed thee in abundance and hath multiplied thy joys. He hath set thee in a safe place; He hath made thee to dwell in the mountain of His grace; He hath covered thee with His mercies. Blessed be His name, for He will surround thee with His presence and satisfy thine heart with His love.

Be not dismayed, neither allow any anxiety to find a nesting place in thy thoughts. For thou art Mine, saith the Lord, and My hand shall protect thee. I will allow no evil to come nigh thee.

Thou art My possession. I shall brook no rivalry. Rebuke the enemy and he shall flee from thee. Count upon My care: I cannot fail. He that keepeth his confidence in Me shall never be disappointed.

This is a solitary walk. This abiding place in Me is completely removed from the multitude; yea, it is a place to be shared with no other — not even thy dearest friend. This knowing Me in secret is an experience alien to the world. This union with Me is the source of thy life, of thy strength, of thy health and vitality. Nothing can substitute.

Prayer is good, but prayer cannot substitute for solitary communion. Fellowship is good, but it is not the source of Life. Life is in Me, and I can give it to thee only in the solitary relationship. Seek that place in Me where no other can intrude. Thou wilt find Me there, and in finding Me thus, ye shall discover all other lacks fulfilled; for in Me there is abundant Life, and with Me there are only joys, and this forever.

Relax Not Thy Vigil

For My people, saith the Lord, lift up thy voice and weep aloud.
    Yea, let thy cry be heard in the night.
    In the stillness, rouse the sleeping.
Say ye to My people, Up, shake thyself from slumber.
    Lay aside thy garments of sleep.
    Gird thyself and put sandals on thy feet.
    Make haste.

Yea, flee to the rock of refuge lest in thy drowsiness, sleeping
        past the hour, thou waken at last to find thyself en-
        snared in the net of the enemy.

For the powers of darkness are about thee on every side.
Yea, he doth not rest in his scheming and plotting.
        For he desireth with an unholy, fiendish delight and
            with bitter, deliberate design,
        to destroy the godly and to break down the building
            of God.

But I have builded My Church, and founded it upon the Rock,
and the very gates of hell shall not prevail against it.

I would not that ye be unaware of his devices;
but having calculated the strength of the opposing force thou
        shalt be moved to see thy need of greater power
            that ye be not overcome.
For My power is available to thee.
Yea, I will Myself fight for thee if thou put thy trust in Me.
        Only relax not thy vigil.
        For they that stumble, stumble in the darkness,
        and they that slumber do so in the night.

        Be thou not overtaken.
Fix thine eyes upon the Sun of Righteousness
        and He shall cause thee to walk in a path of light.

According to Mine Eternal Purposes

Hold thou fast, for lo, I am with thee:
Stand thou still, for I am thy God.
Be thou quiet before Me,
For I have arranged all things for thee according to My good will,
yea, according to Mine eternal purposes.

For I have purposes and plans and desires
which reach far beyond thy present view.
Thou seest as it were the immediate situation,
but My thoughts for thee, and My planning for thee
embraces eternity.
Yea, thou art in My hand.
Rest there, and leave all else to Me.

These Are Days of the Moving of My Spirit

Be alert. Be on guard. Give none offense either to the receptive or the unreceptive; for this changeth from day to day, and the unconcerned today may be the most concerned tomorrow, and vice-versa. Do not attempt to make a judgment as to who is hungry for more of God. At any moment an appetite long dormant may be aroused, and the longer it has been dormant, the more voracious it will be.

Give My Word — My Word alone will whet the appetite. Give ye them to drink. The water shall awaken new thirst. Yea, ye shall say 'How shall I be able to satisfy so great demand?' For these are the days of the moving of My Spirit, saith the Lord; and will ye resist if I wish to make you My aqueduct?

Stay clear — allow no constriction nor obstruction, and be not stingy. There shall spring forth herbage wherever the waters reach.

Give Not Substitutes

My people are hungering for My Word, and when ye are gathered together, I would that ye feed them.

Give not inedible substitutes. Give the lovely bread of the words of Jesus. Yea, spread a feast, and enjoy the delicious and the rich meats of divine truth.

Why should ye hunger when such plenty is at hand? And why should ye be deprived of spiritual nourishment when a table is spread before thee?

Some of the foods may be strange to thee. Despise nothing that I offer thee. Thou needest it, else I would not provide it. Partake of it, even if it is strange to thy taste. Ye will soon come to relish it with delight, and even more so because it *is* a new experience for thee.

Keep thy mind open, else how can ye grow? Fear not deception nor poison. So long as ye seek Me, ye shall be rewarded in finding *Me*. What ye *seek*, that shall ye *find*.

Ye shall not seek bread and find a stone. Ye shall not seek fish and find a scorpion. Ye need have no fear except the fear of a mis-directed quest. Let My Holy Spirit reign in the desires of thy heart, and ye shall be thus guarded from unworthy motives. Let Me keep thy motives free of fleshly lusts and channeled into the paths of righteousness.

Open thine eyes to all I show thee, and open thy mouth wide and let Me fill it as I have promised to do.

Your eyes shall be filled with wonder and your mouth with good things. My words shall come *unto* thee, and My truth shall come forth *from* thee. (I Cor. 14:36)

Stay Beneath My Wing

Thus saith the Lord to His people: Shall I create, and shall I not have it in My power to destroy? Is it not written that the potter breaketh one vessel that He may shape a new one? Shall I not do likewise? Yea, I shall bring My will to pass, and man shall know that his will is as a broken straw when pitted against the Almighty.

But My people shall know the protection of their God. Because their heart is stayed upon Jehovah, therefore shall I keep them in My pavilion and shelter them until the calamity be over-passed.

If I removed thee from the scene, ye would have no testimony of My miraculous delivering power. Stay beneath My wings, and I shall make thee as a tower of strength to which the fearful may run and find safety.

When thou passest through the waters, I will be with thee; and through the rivers, they shall not overflow thee: when thou walkest through the fire, thou shalt not be burned; neither shall the flame kindle upon thee. Isaiah 43:2

Bread Upon the Waters

Be not afraid to follow Me, neither draw back in doubt. For I will provide all that ye are lacking, and I will pave the way for you with My bounty.

Ye are not treading alone. Lo, there are many with thee on the same road. It is the road of faith and trust, and ye shall have sweet fellowship, for there are others who shall join thee in this walk.

Ye shall rejoice with exceeding joy, and thy joy shall be shared by angels. Lo, they walk beside thee and guard thy way.

Never limit Me. I will take thee through, though cliffs should rise before thee. There will always be a provision, and in My mercy I shall see that ye find it.

Be humble and be patient. I am nearer to thee than ye think, and will do more than ye expect. I work in every heart to bring conformity to My word. Ye only need give it. I will do the subsequent work. For My Word is Living and Powerful. It shall not come to failure. It shall accomplish My purpose, though My purpose may be entirely hidden from thee.

So cast thy bread upon the waters, even though they be turbulent flood waters, and it shall return unto thee. (Ec. 11:1)

The Master Artist

Set thy gaze toward heaven. Lo, thine eyes shall behold My glory.

For I have brought thee through the testing time, and My heart rejoiceth over thee. Thou seest but a part of the picture, but I see the design in its completion. Thou canst not know what is in My mind and what I am creating with the materials of thy life.

Only be thou yielded in My hands. Thou needest not to make thine own plans, for I am in control, and thou wouldst bring disaster by interference, even as a child who would wish to help a master artist, and with untrained use of the brush would ruin the canvas.

So rest thy soul, this knowing, that I have been at work, and in ways thou hast least suspected; for the picture in thy thinking and the work with which I was engaged were entirely different.

I make no idle strokes. What I do is never haphazard. I am never merely mixing colors out of casual curiosity. My every move is one of vital creativity, and every stroke is part of the whole.

Never be dismayed by apparent incongruity. Never be alarmed by a sudden dash of color seemingly out of context. Say only to thy questioning heart, 'It is the Infinite wielding His brush; surely He doeth all things well.'

And in all that He does with a free hand, without interference, He can stand back and view the work and say, 'It is good.'

I Am Bringing Sons Into Glory

My people are precious to Me, saith the Lord. No evil shall befall them without My knowledge. My grace have I lavished upon them to conform them to My image. My energies have I given for their nurture and development.

I have not simply brought forth children, but am bringing sons into glory. I have rejoiced in their birth, but rejoice more deeply in their maturity.

Be no more babes, it is written, but GROW. Fed by the Word of God and succored by prayer, let your development into full stature be accomplished.

My hand is upon thee. Draw not back. There may be times when I must wield the rod of correction, but this is for thine ultimate good.

Blessing shall be held back and growth retarded if ye resist My discipline.

Shout the Victory

My people shall be like an army. They shall move at my command and they shall see the victory. I will not send them into an empty valley. I send them against an on-rushing foe, bent on destruction and armed to the teeth with deadly weapons. They shall overcome them, for I shall be their strength, and I shall make the strength of one to be as the strength of ten. I go before and carry the banner.

Shout the victory. Thy God shall respond. He shall even put to flight the armies of the enemy by the sound of His response.

Peace shall come and shall be as a quiet morning and as the stillness of dew.

As the Sounding of the Trumpet

Be patient, My beloved, for the coming of the Lord is at hand. Establish your hearts in Him, and be ye faithful. The Kingdom is at hand, and shall I not make preparation? Yea, I do not have My prophets simply as demonstrations of the miraculous, I have them for the purpose of communicating My message to My people.

Never has it been more needful that they hear Me. It is as vital at this hour as the contact between an army and their commander. Ye dare not risk being cut off. Ye need direction as never before. Ye also need to know the position and strategy of the opponent. This is a cumulative climax. Past battles will be like child's play by comparison. This is an all-out offensive which I am about to launch. Gird up thy loins. Gather up the supplies. Lay aside every hindrance.

My Word shall go forth as the sounding of the trumpet. It shall be clear and distinct. It shall not waver. Many shall hear and be alerted; yea, they who live in the Spirit shall hear, but the dead shall go on about their work as deaf men. No sign shall be given them except the sign of My people being gathered out. The hard of heart, the callous of spirit shall misinterpret and condemn. They shall not see My hand, for it shall be hidden from them. For if they knew the truth they would follow. But I will not allow this, for better that ye be misunderstood than that ye be joined by those whose hearts are unchanged and unprepared.

For My people are a people chosen by Me, saith the Lord. See ye give no heed to the cries of scorn. Close thine ears to all who would detain thee. Cover thy head and run as one who runs for his life. For truly not thy life only, but the lives of thy children are at stake. Be as deaf to other men as they are deaf to Me.

Surely I am doing a work of righteousness, yea, even in the earth. For I say unto thee, ye are not of the world, even though

ye are in the world. I will wash thy feet and cleanse thee from
the defilement of the way. I will fit thee to walk in a path of holiness. I will put away false doctrine, and ye shall hear truth. Ye
shall eat the good of the land. Ye shall flourish and be made
fruitful, saith the Lord.

Because ye have sought Me, I will bless you; yea, I will
stand in your midst. I will even joy over thee with singing.

Ye Shall Come Forth as Gold

Thus saith the Lord, I know the way that ye take, and when
thou comest forth, ye shall come forth as gold, yea, as pure gold,
having been tried in the fire. For Mine eye is upon thee in loving
watchfulness, and Mine ear is open to thy cry.

Be not over-charged with anxiety. I am thy burden-bearer.
Be not anxious for the morrow, for on the morrow I shall be thy
sure supply. Praise Me NOW, and let thy confidence in Me be
manifest. So shall the faith of others be encouraged, for thy life
is a witness to many.

The Lord is thy portion: He shall keep thee in peace. Because ye have made the Most High thy abiding place, He shall
deliver thee in trouble. He shall bless thee and reward thee, and
reveal to thee the greatness of His salvation.

I Shall Come Singing

My children, be silent before Me that I may speak to you. I will lift up My voice as the sound of a trumpet — I will speak clearly to you, for the hour is at hand.

Be obedient, and raise thy standards of discipline and dedication to a higher level. For My face is set toward My soon-return to earth. I wait only the release from the Father's hand. Yea, I long to come, and to be united with My chosen ones; but the Father holdeth the times in His own power.

And I say unto thee, that though I am ready and longing to come unto thee, yea, would have rejoiced to have come much sooner, lo, I say to thee, thou art not yet ready. I have wooed thee and I have warned thee. Ye have spurned My entreaties, and ye have fought against the restrainings of the Spirit.

Break through your religious curtain, and behold Me in My glory. Keep thy vision filled with Me. Keep thy life in tune and thy worship in mutual harmony.

For I shall come singing, and what will ye if ye be in dischord?

Expect the Unexpected

O My child, let Me speak to thee, and let My Spirit direct thy life. I may lead you in unexpected ways, and ask things of you that are startling, but I will never guide you amiss.

Across thy path shall fall the shadow of My hand, and wheresoever I direct thee, there shall ye see My power at work, and there shall come forth from thy ministry that which shall glorify Me.

Do not walk according to thy natural reasonings, but obey the promptings of the Spirit, and be obedient to My voice.

I need those who will be completely flexible in this way, because there are a multitude of souls who are searching for Me, and would never come into contact with Me in a personal way through the channels of the organized church.

Ye shall go as Philip went — at the behest of the Spirit — into the places that are out of the way, and bring light on My Word to those who are in need.

Stay in an attitude of prayer and faith, and I will do all the rest.

Eternal Destiny of the Present Moment

O My child, it is not appointed unto thee to know the future, nor to be able to discern aforetime My exact plans. It is enough that we should walk together in love and trust. No doubts need mar thy peace, nor anxieties cloud thy brow. Rest in the knowledge that My ways are perfect and My grace is all-sufficient. Ye shall find My help is adequate, no matter what may befall.

Let none say to thee, 'Lo, this shall be, or that shall verily come to pass'. Live, rather, in the awareness of the eternal destiny of the present moment. To be unduly occupied with matters of the future is to thine own disadvantage. So much is waiting to be done NOW.

It is written: 'Occupy till I come'. Live according to this injunction. Thy life is in My hands. I can only use what is available to Me at the moment. Others need guidance and help with their present problems. Minister in the realm of the here and now, and thou shalt have much fruit in the day of reaping.